The Journal of Unemployment Studies

The Journal of Unemployment Studies

Celia Scher Wagner

Jane - thank you for keeping me going! - Celia

ISBN 978-0-557-53508-8

Contents

December Through February

I took a sabbatical. It had been thirty years since I'd had a long stretch of time off, and I was worn out and sad, and in mourning for my career, and I just wanted to regroup, and I didn't have the heart to job hunt. I thought I would write down everything I had learned about being a manager, and I wrote 120 pages. That seemed to about cover it. I didn't really organize it in any way. I talked to one friend about publishing it, and then decided I had been a little too frank, and besides, I was done with books. So I set it aside.

After a while, it occurred to me that I needed some kind of Event with which to mark the end of the sabbatical and the beginning of the job search. I decided if I ever got behind a desk again, I would kick myself hard if I hadn't enjoyed my time off while I had it. In the great scheme of life, I knew I was in a "time but no income" phase, after having been in an "income but no time" phase for ages. So—what should I do?

I should get something checked off the life list. I had never been to Yosemite or the Grand Canyon. I would go. I would stay in the lodges, if possible. Every time I told my friends of my planned road trip, they would begin ladling on additional sights: If I was going to do that, then I really had to see Death Valley. If I was going to do that, I really had to see Zion. If I was going to do that, I really had to see Bryce Canyon. . . .

It turned out some of the lodges and roads weren't open until March. Okay. I would take a Big Drive in March.

It was a plan! I would not even start looking for a job until after the Big Drive. And I would come back, and start hunting on April Fool's Day. I had to start sometime. That seemed like an auspicious date.

March

The Big Drive

- 4,000 miles
- 8 national parks and lots of other scenic and cultural wonders:
  - ✓ Ashland (a play for $10—the economy had everybody scared)
  - ✓ Mount Shasta
  - ✓ San Francisco with the Togasakis and Besh
  - ✓ Yosemite with Besh
  - ✓ Death Valley
  - ✓ Hoover Dam, the Grand Canyon, and Zion with Julie
  - ✓ Valley of Fire
  - ✓ Bryce Canyon
  - ✓ Grand Staircase–Escalante National Monument
  - ✓ Capitol Reef
  - ✓ Arches
  - ✓ Mesa Verde
  - ✓ The Painted Hills
- 8 states:
  - ✓ Oregon
  - ✓ California
  - ✓ Nevada
  - ✓ Colorado
  - ✓ Utah

- ✓ New Mexico
- ✓ Arizona
- ✓ Idaho

Soundtrack: *The Magnificent Westerns* (4-CD set, thanks to Ron Wessner for the loan)

April Through July

The Goal, the Method, the Landmarks

My friend and former CFO, Gary, said that if I wanted to change industries, I would have to meet 100 people.

This is the sort of thing Gary would say. It's clear and quantifiable.

He also gave me a process: Make a notebook. Each person I meet gets a page in the notebook: Name, address, phone, e-mail, date we met, who introduced us, who he or she introduced me to, and what I want to remember from the meeting. Four weeks later, I re-contact each person to say, "Hello, I'm still out here, just in case you've had a thought about some job that might fit me."

I have followed pieces of this advice. The easier part turned out to be the quest to meet 100 people.

Though I correspond with Gary pretty frequently, I have avoided clarifying what "meet" actually means. Does he mean they have to be strangers? If so, I have a ways to go. If not, I'm doing pretty well. Also, I've decided a meeting has to last 20 minutes or more. A handshake and exchange of cards doesn't count.

- The goal: Get a job in a new industry.
- The method: Meet 100 people, make a notebook . . .
- The landmarks:
  - ✓ Get interview clothes.
  - ✓ Meet one person, ask for additional contacts.
  - ✓ Meet with people (some of whom you may already know).
  - ✓ Meet new people.

- ✓ Fix your resume.
- ✓ Apply for a job.
- ✓ Apply for unemployment.
- ✓ Actually contact somebody a month after you met and say, “I’m still out here.”
- ✓ Volunteer someplace you’d like to work.
- ✓ Join a networking group.
- ✓ Attend a semi-serious networking function.
- ✓ Attend a networking mixer.
- ✓ Get an actual JOB interview, not an informational interview.
- ✓ Get a second job interview.
- ✓ Prove yourself useful to someone else.

Business Cards

I didn’t know what I should put as my title/desired role/specialization.

Operations? Project management? Process improvement? Business analysis?

Fortunately, I read an article that said if you don’t know what to put, then just skip that part. Get your name, phone, and e-mail on there, so you can start handing them out.

I took a photo I liked (the one of two spirits holding hands with two people, from Valley of Fire State Park, which I’d found on the Big Drive in March) down to Office Depot. Heather Jean was behind the counter. Saints be praised! Heather Jean turns out to be a graphic arts wizard. I asked her if she could turn the photo into my business card background. She looked thoughtful, then said, “Can I have overnight?”

Yes. You may.

They were the best biz cards ever. They were a great topic of conversation. I loved them. Almost everybody else did, too.

FENG, TANG, DANG, WING, GONG*

Networking Group haiku:

Unemployed former

Execs must advise me, yet

They too have no job.

Speaking of which . . .

Et Tu, Mom haiku:

I advise daughter

On how to job hunt, and yet

I too have no job.

State of Oregon Unemployment Training

I put it off as long as I could, but finally I applied for unemployment and went to the mandatory training session. Just like the Greyhound station, a little slice of Americana, all of us in the same boat, laboring over our computer terminals, signing up, searching the job postings, taking an online Math test, taking an online Comprehension test, practicing this and that.

The lady next to me reached a place in her application where it asked if she could run a postage meter. She was fretting over this—she had done it, but maybe 15 years ago, and she doubted she could run a newfangled one today. I assured her she could. Really. It would take her ten minutes to learn how. She was dubious.

I thought I had filled in the online resume, but it turned out I'd skipped a section. The unemployment training guy was looking over my shoulder, and he said, "You didn't fill in Education." I typed in Yale as my college, and he became dramatic and overly solicitous: "You went to YALE, oh NO, and YOU have no job, that's TERRIBLE."

---

* FENG = FINANCIAL EXECUTIVES NETWORKING GROUP; TANG = THE APPAREL NETWORKING GROUP; DANG = DANA A'S NETWORKING GROUP, WING = WOMEN IN NETWORKING GROUPS; GONG = GROUPS OF NETWORKING GROUPS. OKAY, I MADE UP THE LAST TWO.

There was something creepy about this, a whiff of schadenfreude. I tried to dodge the spotlight: “Hey, look, lots of people have no job, it’s okay, it will all work out.” Then he and his colleague settled in to help me fix the resume, tighten it up, make it shorter. They wanted me to “look thirty-eight on paper.” I should leave off the dates of my first jobs. In fact, maybe I should leave Yale off? I might get a job quicker that way!

“Can I ask you something personal?” the guy said. “Why did you go to Yale?”

“I fell in love with it.”

“What was your major?”

“English.”

He laughed. “At least it wasn’t Art History! But that would have been if you went to Brown.”

I went home and sulked and wrote my wing-woman Karin a whiny note. She said she’d gone to the unemployment training too, and it made her want to poke her eyes out. So succinct, that Karin.

The Ladders ’n’ Me:
The Passive-Aggressive Voice

My friend Jill said I should try TheLadders.com as a job-hunting site, so I sent in my $29.95 and signed up. Right off the bat, I got an offer of a free resume critique. I uploaded my resume and awaited the news.

The news arrived the next morning. It seemed about seven pages long, and was prefaced by a raft of baloney along the lines of, Here at TheLadders, we take only the cream of the unemployed crop, and you were lucky enough to be allowed to send us your $29.95. You are a formerly hard-charging biz person, so I don’t need to sugar-coat anything for you. If something isn’t working optimally, you want to know about it!

The rest of the missive basically said, *Your resume stinks*.

There were, of course, subheads. Your resume stinks because you formatted it wrong. Your resume stinks because you used old language. Your resume stinks because it doesn’t grab the reader.

Within each of these subheads, they had pulled out little bits and phrases that best exemplified the powerful stinkiness of my particular resume. After a few pages, I began to suspect the seven pages were a template with blanks to be filled in. Perhaps everybody got seven pages, lightly customized. Perhaps the folks at TheLadders slogged through every resume fishing for tidbits to toss under each subhead, and voila—a seven-page resume critique!

Let me just say that I didn't much like my resume, either. Really, I didn't. I thought it sounded weird and false and full of meaningless biz-speak. Still, the critique was deflating.

Near the middle, though, I began to move from deflated to nettled. It was in the subhead called *"The passive voice."* This little section said, in a condescending tone, something like this: *You probably haven't thought about the passive voice since high school, but here at TheLadders, we make it our business to think about absolutely everything that makes a resume zingy, and the passive voice is not it. You used the passive voice. You mustn't do that. It's a dreadful thing to do. Busy HR people don't have time for this sort of thing. Your resume will get deleted in seconds and you will stay unemployed for a long, long time. You need professional help! You used the passive voice in the phrase, 'consulted with.'*

Well, no.

In the seven pages, there were no suggestions for improvement. Suggestions are not free. Instead, there was an offer at the end for me to get my resume professionally rewritten, for just under $700. And there was a signature, from somebody with an arch-preppy name like (but not really) Whitney Smythe-Pendleton III.

(Interestingly, Whitney wanted me to know that he-or-she would not rewrite my resume. Some professional rewriter would do that. I suspect I am not the first person to take a deep dislike to my critiquer.)

I knew, truly I did, that this message was not meant to begin a correspondence. But they had hit an English-major nerve, and I was cranky. I wrote back.

"Dear Whitney," said I, "strangely enough, I have thought about the passive voice since high school, and 'consulted with' is not it.

'Consulted with' is the beginning of a prepositional phrase, pure and simple. Sincerely yours."

The next morning, my phone rang. "It's Whitney," said the voice on the other end.

"Whitney!" I said. "You are a person! I thought you were a program! Huh. What can I do for you?"

Whitney offered me a price break. For me, this week only, a special: just under 600 bucks.

I said no. Then I went out and paid somebody else to help me rewrite my resume. I liked her. I never found a job on TheLadders.com that suited me, either.

August

I was going for a communications job, and they wanted the candidates to have experience using modern social networking media, such as blogging. I thought, *Okay, I will have a blog, then.* I threw a whole bunch of stuff together so that it would appear the blog had several pages. I figured I'd just sort of whip through it, if necessary. No potential employer ever asked to see it, so no harm done. But it was fun, so I kept going.

Things to Worry About

From TheLadders:

"Is Your Life Story Boring?"

I Searched for "Unemployment Poetry" but the Rhymes Were Awful Haiku

Why does a search on

"Business analyst" bring back

Nanny Wanted ad?

Hey, Guys, Let's Put On a Summit!

Headline from discussion group on LinkedIn:

"National Summit on Business-to-Business Arbitration still has room for in-house counsel with considerable experience with business-to-business arbitration."

But Mo-ommmmm…!

One of those wondrous keyword-inspired sidebar ads on Gmail:

"Get your next job using your resume, not your cleavage!"

Informal Poll on the Prevalence of Finance Recruiters

After a while, as I was on the quest to meet 100 people in Portland, the trend became pretty obvious. So I started asking folks for their opinion on the following: Why have I (so far) met many recruiters and placement folks who say, "I specialize in placing Finance people," but none who specialize in placing Ops people?

Theories advanced by people I've met:

- It's not a random sample. I just haven't yet met the Ops recruiters.
- When a company is in trouble, the bearer of bad news is the Finance person. Companies tend to trade in their bearer of bad news and get a new one. Given the amount of bad news in today's economy, there is a lot of churn in high-level CFO types.
- Companies switch CFOs regularly. The average tenure of a CFO right now (according to a local Finance recruiter) is 28 months.
- Companies are in the habit of going to agencies to find Finance people. Everybody does it. There are a lot of such agencies. But HR people look for Ops people within their own industry and think they can do it themselves, without using an agency. They don't feel that way about Finance jobs.
- Every single company needs a Finance person, and it's a specialized skill set. There are simply more opportunities to place Finance people.
- Finance people are very factual by nature, not given to hype, and don't market themselves well, so they need recruiters. In contrast, Sales & Marketing people, and HR people, can sell themselves, so they don't need recruiters. (This doesn't explain the dearth of operations recruiters. My sense is that we're pretty factual and low on hype, too.)
- Finance people's skills are more or less interchangeable (so a search for one is, in the words of a placement person, "scalable."). They have similar training (though some have

more than others). They are commodities. It's easy for a recruiter to do a search and find what she is looking for.

- It's easy to place Finance people (Note: Finance recruiters dispute this! One Finance recruiter says burger companies want only burger Finance guys.)
- Okay, it's not easy to place Finance people. But it's easier to place them than Ops people.
- Operations is a broad term. Finance is defined.
- Finance people used to run one-fifth of the economy. They were well paid. Since recruiters get a portion of the pay for people they place, recruiters wanted to place them.
- The financial sector was, until recently, growing. A lot of placement people were needed. Now that Finance has shrunk, there are excess Finance recruiters.
- Getting a CPA got harder when they added a fifth year requirement. Finance people switch from public accounting to private right around the time they are "seniors" (but not yet managers). There actually is a shortage of seniors. (A former Finance recruiter).

Today's Fortune Cookie

. . . honestly, said:

"You will have good luck in the autumn."

It did not specify the autumn of which year.

Networking Failure Haiku

Fan Starbuck site says

There is a shop on Ninth and

Park. But Ninth is Park.

Today's Brow-Furrower

From a sidebar ad along with my EarthLink bill:

"[This application] lets you send e-mail to loved ones who don't use the Internet. Your e-mail messages (plus attachments, such as photos) are automatically printed out as attractive, easy-to-read letters. . . ."

Excellent Suggestion!

Friend Julie says that without her glasses, she thought the name of the blog was actually The Journal o' Funemployment Studies.

Wow. What a good idea!

(Back in my library supply days, I could have changed the title and then made an in-joke about having done so. Serials librarians used to go absolutely ape whenever a serial publication decided to rename itself. I treasured an old link to a rant written in *rhyming couplets* about serial name changes, but the link stopped working this year. Considering all the junk that lives forever on the web, this is pretty annoying. The perpetrator of this mini-crime will answer to me someday!

Anyway, I suspect that in these latter, post-card-catalog days, name changes no longer cause much concern in library-land, but back in the laborious cross-reference times, they caused much sighing.)

Sunday's Brow-Furrower

Of course, it would be Sunday.

Bumper sticker spotted in the New Seasons parking lot:

"I'm against the death penalty.

Look what happened to Jesus."

Walden-Wear: When You Really Need to Focus

Thoreau, expounding on the virtue of economy in Walden, gets all sniffy about the beauty and worthiness of old clothes, how "old clothes will serve a hero," how "only they who go to soirees and legislative balls must have new coats." And then he winds up with that admonition we've all heard the first half of: "I say, beware of all enterprises that require new clothes, and not rather a new wearer of clothes."

It's a resonant and altogether Biblical line, and I can only imagine he was pleased with it. But if he meant it, then it tells me two things:

Thoreau was definitely a guy, and

Thoreau was not job hunting.

Nonetheless, there's a kernel in there for today's job hunter. And this is it: Do not interview wearing an outfit that required you to purchase new and unusual underwear. For that matter, do not present to any group, even if you are employed, wearing new and unusual underwear. New is okay, and my friend Bonnie swears it is necessary, but "unusual" is fatal.

In late summer 2001, we were gearing up for our annual sales meeting, the biggest event of our corporate year. I got some snazzy new clothes which (I felt) necessitated new and unusual underwear. Specifically, I bought my first (and last) thong. I was scheduled to present on September 12, the second day of the meeting.

Yes, that means that September 11, 2001, was the first day of the meeting. I was driving to work that morning, and turned on the car radio, and I had missed a big chapter of something awful, but I couldn't tell what. I got to the hotel where we were meeting and joined the group around the lobby TV. We were all stunned. And then eventually we went into the meeting room, where our leader said that people had flown in from all over the world for this meeting, they had nowhere to go, it was fine if anyone couldn't attend or had to leave the room, but . . . we were going to try to go ahead and hold the meeting as planned, because we could do nothing else. So we went ahead.

People spoke on the first day, but it was a blur. The evening was a blur. September 12, I got up and put on my new thong under my new duds. The show would go on, and like everyone else, I was operating on automatic. I gave my presentation, and I was distracted, like everyone else. But my secret shame was that I was distracted by the unfolding story of the airplanes and extra-distracted by the fact that my underwear was making me more uncomfortable than I had been since childbirth. I knew I was a shallow and insensitive person, or maybe shallow and overly sensitive. But my inability to ignore the local and (extremely) personal in the face of national tragedy seemed a huge failing.

Today, on the job-hunt trail, I attended an all-day class. It was in the same room of the same hotel, almost exactly 8 years later. I walked into that room and began to squirm. But the teacher was good, and after a couple of hours, I got over it. I have an interview next week. I am determined not to go shopping before then.

Confidential Job Posting—Shhhhh!

Spotted on a local job board:

"Confidential

FLORAL DESIGNER—Shop experience required. Contact Delyhlia at 503–639–6. . . ."

I thought the point of a confidential posting was to obscure the hiring entity, and maybe also not to alert the incumbent that she was about to be replaced. I thought confidential postings either said "Contact this recruiter . . ." or they said, "Please send your resume to 'Mr. Jones' at P.O. Box ##."

I apparently do not grasp the point of "confidential." Or these people don't.

September

Today's Most Amazing Lists

Here is "Seattle Interview Coach" reporting on a study in CareerCast.com.

- Best Cities to Find a Job (August 2009)
  - ✓ Riverside, CA
  - ✓ Detroit
  - ✓ Memphis
  - ✓ Louisville
  - ✓ Tampa Bay
  - ✓ St. Louis
  - ✓ Cincinnati
  - ✓ Phoenix
- Worst Cities to Find a Job (August 2009)
  - ✓ Riverside, CA
  - ✓ Detroit
  - ✓ Memphis
  - ✓ Louisville
  - ✓ Tampa Bay
  - ✓ St. Louis
  - ✓ Cincinnati
  - ✓ Phoenix

Only English Majors Need Apply . . .

A Headline in The Southeast Examiner*, September 2009:*

“Couplet and Sewer Project Underway”

Dear Hiring Manager:

My thoughts upon the sewer

Are nothing if not pu-ure.

What do you think? Huh?

Sincerely yours,

One, Zero, One Hundred . . .
One Hundred and Fifty

Faithful readers know that my old buddy Gary told me to meet 100 people, if I wanted to find a new industry/job in Portland.

The trouble with the job hunt is that it’s hard on those of us who are basically incremental types. The job hunt is not visibly incremental. It’s binary—you have one job, or zero jobs.

For a while, I got snotty and defensive when friends asked me how it was going, because hey, I had zero jobs, that was how it was going. But then I found that a better answer was, “I have met (so many) out of my 100 people, so I’m getting closer.”

(Assuming that I shall find a job, then by definition, every day I am getting closer to it. Of course, I’m getting closer to being dead every day, and that one is guaranteed. Be careful what you measure. Loose association about reasoning: There’s the widely bruited theory that you have to look one month for every $10,000 you will make, so if you want to make $100K, it will take you 10 months of searching. Rick, with his keen nose for fallacies, has joked that I should just look for a REALLY LONG time, as that will surely lead to a giant salary.)

But I digress.

Last week the leader of Career Camp (yes, I am going to Career Camp) said that my friend Gary used to be right, but now it’s 150 people.

I have mixed feelings about this news. On the one hand, meeting people has been an absolute delight, and now that I can see 100 on the horizon, I can work up to a little sadness that someday the variety of my days could diminish. On the other hand, wow, okay, the goal is 150, so . . . deep breath, I'm not really getting close yet. Darn. Pretty soon, the new people I meet will suggest I meet somebody back up the chain, and then I will have looped all of Portland.

And here's something else that wasn't exactly what I had in mind. Today, on an interview, I told the hiring manager about my meet-100-people sub-goal, and at the end of the interview, she thanked me warmly for that great idea, and said she was going to suggest it to other job seekers.

No problem. I was just sort of hoping the end of the interview would have a little hint of, "We would love to work with you," as opposed to, "Thanks for the great advice to job seekers." It's much like the networking group conundrum—I enjoy my networking group buds, and find them a huge source of support. But I don't want to become "a networking ANIMAL," as one of the guys described another, as a pure and isolated art form.

Can't be helped, though. High achievers in a binary bind are going to do something. We're all high achievers. Watch us find a way to achieve.

Not Really News. It Was Ever Thus.

. . . from the Portland Business Journal:

"Employers say top talent hard to find.

"Despite the growing number of professionals finding themselves suddenly out of work and back in the job market, employers aren't having an easy time getting the best candidate.

"A study of 501 hiring managers by Menlo Park-Calif. based Robert Half and CareerBuilder found that 44% of resumes received by hiring managers come from unqualified applicants."

Well, sure, maybe the *hiring managers* think those are unqualified applicants.

I am reminded of the time one of my science buddies got a cover letter from a young fellow who had been working in a bakery, and who felt that made him a great lab tech candidate. The cover letter began, "I love yeast."

Seven Industries I Don't Want to Work in Next

- Alcohol
- Tobacco
- Firearms
- Porn
- Gambling
- Spam
- Bookselling

I Guess I Won't Ask Dad to LinkIn With Me

I saw on LinkedIn that the college-age daughter of one of my 100 Generous-and-Helpful People had interned at a place I'd love to work. I asked the mom if she'd connect me to her daughter, so that maybe I could ask a corporate culture question or two, or just find out how to dress for the interview.

The mom said sure, but she should tell me a bit about her daughter first. "She goes to Berkeley," said the mom. "She decided when she was eight that she was going to Berkeley, and she goes there now. I asked her when she made that announcement at eight, 'Why Berkeley?' She said it was because they had protest marches. I asked her what she wanted to protest, and she said, 'Doesn't matter.'"

I digested this briefly, then asked the mom what I should wear to the interview. She gave me great advice.

Practice, Practice, Practice Interviewing Still Won't Get You to Carnegie Hall

Yesterday, out of the kindness of their hearts, eight HR people came to one of my networking groups, and we divided up, two HR people, two job seekers, and did some practice interviews. This turned out to be enormous fun. I got to watch my fellow job seeker, Brad, answer questions. I have interviewed many, many people. I have (now) been through a fair number of interviews. But I haven't watched anybody else get interviewed.

I kept thinking, wow, I can't have a personality transplant and actually become Brad, but I could add to my range, take a few leaves from his book.

Where I told exciting stories, Brad told calming stories. There's a thought! Where I was forceful, Brad was philosophical. Where I rushed in, Brad pondered. I'd hire me in a minute, of course, but I'd hire Brad, too.

And then we got feedback, from the two HR people, and from the other job seeker. And that part was good, too. As somebody pointed out, we've all been on a bunch of interviews, but we rarely get any feedback from them. (Thank you now to Doug, who walked me to the lobby after that one panel interview, and muttered that I'd done fine, and been the best prepared of all candidates.) I was in a particularly congenial little group, and we ended up laughing and drinking beer together, so it was a fun exercise.

How strange then, that the e-mail this morning from one of my many job-hunt lists sounded like an awful idea. For only a small fee, an HR professional offered to have you send him your resume and a list of the questions you were asked at the last interview where you didn't get the job. Over the phone, he would then conduct a mock 20- to 30-minute interview, at the end of which he would tell you why you didn't get the job.

Does he sport a long, fringe-y shawl while doing this? Does he keep the lights low, and gaze into a crystal ball?

I will concede that perhaps some of us just blow interviews over and over, and need to make some fundamental adjustments. But I also know that many times when I was hiring, it wasn't so much that a candidate blew it, as that several candidates shone. Many, many times—most times—it was a close call. No stranger on the telephone repeating my questions would ever have known why I didn't hire a given candidate. The gall!

This little service gives me a bad feeling—it's too near an occasion to prey on people's insecurities, or just kick them when they're down.

Why Don't You Stay Home and Paint the Sistine Chapel, Then?

Good days on the job hunt are days when you make a genuine connection. Right now, a day when somebody says, "I wish we were hiring, because we would love to have you," is a good day. It's not a day when you found work, but it's still good, it still puts you on your feet, it's strength for the journey.

Bad days are when somebody gets you wrong, or the connection is full of static.

The first bad day was the fellow who looked at me, sighed, and said, "Oh, why don't you just retire? Stay home and paint." (And please let me hasten to add that this gentleman of wealth and influence was a good deal older than I am.) He then grilled me at length on why I didn't just retire. Was I greedy? Couldn't we get by on Rick's salary? Didn't I have hobbies?

I did pretty well in his presence (in fact, I kept him the entire allotted half hour, because he ticked me off—and I did get him to talk about work, and even to laugh), but he deflated me pretty badly for a few days. The fun part was the end, when he said, "I don't meet many women like you," and I got to say, "Huh. Why do you suppose that is?"

Last week, a kind woman in pearls was full of good tips, but ended our interview by suggesting I consider whether God just didn't want me to work.

That sounded an awful lot like, "Why don't you just retire?" and it felt like a sucker punch. But I've chewed on it long enough to puzzle it out: She was saying (a) I've got free time right now; it's a gift; and I should try to enjoy it while I have it; and (b) when it's supposed to happen, it will happen, so I should be easy on myself.

At least, that's what I want her to have been saying. I don't know.

Ecosystem Moments, Part 1

After the helpful HR people came to my networking group and did the practice interviews with us, I went up and thanked one of them for giving us her time. "You do this all day," I said, "and now you came and did it for us, too, for free, out of the goodness of your heart. That was so generous of you."

"Are you kidding?" she said. "I love interviewing people. Do you know how long it's been since I got to interview anyone? We've had a hiring freeze on for 8 months."

The day my job ended, before I drove home, I went by the dry cleaner's across the street from the office, picked up my stuff, and gave them back their clothes bag.

"Not dropping off?" said the lady behind the counter.

"No," said I. "I lost my job, and I don't live nearby, so I'm just giving you back your bag."

Tears sprang into her eyes.

I was feeling pretty tearful myself, but this reaction surprised me. We were not dear friends—I was a customer; she was the nice lady behind the counter.

And then I thought: Oh, right. You and I do exchange pleasantries every ten days or so, we have talked about the weather, and once you told a story about your elderly parents going out to the store in their pajamas that I will always treasure—but those tears aren't because you are going to miss me. Those tears are: another customer gone.

The whole job-hunting/dating analogy has its place, and has its limits as well. I've got a crush on this one organization, for instance, and have now interviewed there five times—two informational, two for a job I didn't get (though I'm assured I was close); and the last one with a really great HR person who said I was just their sort; she knew there would be a place for me there; it was only a matter of time and endurance.

I went home from that one feeling buoyant, and last week I related it to a group of fellow job hunters: "No, nothing yet, but So-and-So, at Organization X, said I was just their sort, there would be a place for me, it was only a matter of time."

"Oooh, good luck!" said Maggie. "But you know, she says that to everybody."

I stuffed my fingers into my ears. "Don't tell me that!"

"Sorry, sorry!" said Maggie. "She did say it to another friend of mine, though."

(Well, heck—why can't two of us be just their sort? It's a big enough place. I am more than willing to share.)

Transparency Would Be Nice

A good friend sent me a link to a job, and though it was on my "7-least-wanted" industries list, I applied out of a sense that I should, because he had been so kind as to send it to me.

After a good deal of interviewing, it turned out to pay lots less than unemployment, with a very sketchy "commission" on top. I withdrew my name, and sent the good friend a note.

He answered that he too had been offered the job (I didn't even know he was applying for it!), and had turned it down because of the pay. This must happen often to the fellow making the offer. Why does he not say up front what the pay is, and save wear and tear on himself and others? Both my friend and I were drained by the whole episode, and the guy with the job must be drained too, over and over. He finds somebody promising, he invests time and energy in that person, and it's all for nothing. He's going to end up with a newly minted worker or someone who is otherwise financially supported, so why not just post the salary, and let those folks apply?

For that matter, why doesn't everybody just say what jobs pay? Surely we waste enormous time with this dance. I know of a woman who spent months interviewing for a job, only to be offered much less than she'd stated she needed from the very beginning. What was that about?

Today's Most Easily Resisted Suggestions

Bumper sticker, a la the common "Keep Portland Weird," but instead:

"Keep San Antonio Lame"

Ad in Tails magazine at the vet's office:

"Give your pet SoftNails!"

(Photo of small, fluffy white dog, head cocked, red ribbon in topknot, false toenails (!!) in alternating red and black.)

Bumper sticker, black block letters on yellow, single word:

"VACUUM"

Application to the Hotel California, Part 1

You can check out anytime you like,

But you can never leave.

Or, in the case of this organization: You can apply any time you like, but you can't fill in the application and send it to us.

I can open up a nice PDF file application form, but I can't type anything into it. I can put the cursor anywhere I want, but that's about it. The cursor blinks blithely, I tap the keys, nothing happens.

Dear Hiring Manager:

I would love to work for your organization, but I can't actually fill in the application. I can't be the only one. Why a PDF?

Sincerely. . . .

I sent the hiring manager an e-mail. What the heck. It began, "Okay, I am beyond embarrassment. . . ." Next, I'll print the thing off, fill it out in crayon, and mail it to him. That should brighten his day.

Long ago, on an all-night road trip, we hit a moment when "Hotel California" was playing on every radio station. Honest. That was pretty scary, too.

I Was Once Good With Names

The goal of meeting 100 people (now 150 people) was to expand my Portland network, but it turns out I know people around town. I ran into a checker from my old Safeway in a Thai restaurant, for instance. I ran into a woman who'd been in a production of *Fiddler* that I'd choreographed. She signed me in when I went to donate blood at the Red Cross.

And I run into former colleagues. I'm in two job-search networking groups, both pretty small. A few months ago, lo and behold, a former colleague showed up in one group—(let's call him) Thomas, who used to manage IT. Thomas got laid off last year, several months before me. He was a nice guy—quiet, calm, almost professorial—with a beautiful mane of pure white hair; white beard; soft-spoken, thoughtful manner; analytical. It was nice to see Thomas again.

Then I missed one or two meetings, or he did. Maybe he had landed a job.

I showed up late for this week's meeting, and I had to laugh, because of all things, there was a new face at the table, and he was yet another former-colleague-IT-guy. I couldn't remember his name, and he had changed a lot over the years. He must have put on weight, because his face was much rounder than it used to be. He had twinkly eyes and dark hair, very shiny and perfectly cut, like a seal pelt. In fact, the terrific haircut made up for the rounder face—he seemed to have aged not at all, just to have gotten a round face. He smiled, I smiled back, but the meeting had started, so I couldn't say hi and welcome him to the group. I was racking my brain. What was his NAME? It bugged me that I could remember he was an IT guy, but I couldn't remember his name.

What a strange filing system my brain uses. I once was in the lunchroom early, and a programmer came in to get coffee, and though we'd worked together for ages, I wasn't wide awake and I just couldn't recall his name either . . . but I DID know he had one of those Hungarian last names where there's a whole syllable without any vowels in it. I managed to say, "Hey, how's it going?" but what my brain was prompting me to say was, "Hi, person without enough vowels in your last name!"

Fortunately, back at the networking group, we were going around the table introducing ourselves and giving our spiels, and the new member was going to give his name before me. So I could wait and I'd know the answer. I was pulling up little bits of info from the dark recesses: He wasn't just an IT guy; he was a nice IT guy. I liked working with him. He had a pleasant and easy-going temper . . .

I kept racking, racking, not listening to the people who were going before him, and then it was his turn, and he said, “Hello, my name is Thomas, and . . .”

Oh.

Moon face comes from no more beard. Dark hair comes from the same place my dark hair comes from. Thomas was filed under white hair and white beard. I couldn’t recognize him.

- Number of men I know who are dyeing their hair as of today: 2
- Percentage of those men who are unemployed: 100%
- Number of women I know who are dyeing their hair as of today: uncountable
- Percentage of those women who are unemployed: small

Application to the Hotel California, Part 2

You will recall that the HC application wanted me to fill in a PDF, and I couldn’t do it. I left out the fact that the website asked me to fill in the PDF (click here, etc.), and then e-mail it to a certain person.

The response to my “I am beyond embarrassment message” began, “I still hold you in high regard.”

That was nice.

Then my correspondent told me it was okay that I couldn’t type into the PDF, because I wasn’t supposed to. I was supposed to print it, fill it in by hand, and mail it via snail mail. (No mention of whether using crayon was okay or not.)

So, good! I wasn’t crazy. It couldn’t be done! But, said I, “there was only an e-mail address on the website. So . . . where to snail mail it?”

“Good point!” said my correspondent. He’d fix that right away.

Who’s her own little worst enemy, then? I mean, now everybody who wants to apply will actually know how! I could have kept my mouth shut. Plus, no doubt my correspondent is tired of me already.

Once, years ago, I had this blissfully uninterrupted day, which ended with an irate colleague showing up at my desk and telling me my phone was off the hook. Really? It didn't look that way, but yes, it was just a little bit crooked in the cradle. Oops.

I wonder if the Hotel California hiring folks had noticed that few applications were coming in?

Ecosystem Moments, Part 2

In the most well-appointed office I have visited yet, someone said, "I think the economic contraction has been good for people. They've gotten rid of their gardeners, and they are doing their own gardening. They've gotten rid of their dog walkers, and they are getting out into the neighborhood with their dogs."

I thought, Ohhh, dear, not my ecosystem.

- I don't know anybody who matches this description, and
- So, in the phrase "good for people," by "people" we mean: not-gardeners, and not-dog-walkers?

Candidate Must Provide Own Sword

pdxMindShare.com Job Postings haiku:

Job description asks

for a ninja or Jedi.

Boy-speak! Code is war.

When I Knew I Wasn't Going to Get Hired at Nike

I drove out to Nike the Friday before my interview, to make sure I wouldn't get lost on the day. I wanted to check how long it would take to get there, how hard it would be to park, and where the building was, on that famously giant campus.

I scheduled the trial run at my leisure, and Highway 26 at 10:30 on a Friday morning was not crowded. Parking was a breeze; signage to the building was clear. Trial run success!

The campus is as beautiful as you may have heard. It was so gorgeous, I took a walk, justifying it as a reconnaissance mission, scoping out what people were wearing so I could dress appropriately for the interview. One Nike friend had said not to wear a suit. "When we see people in suits, we know they are consultants." Another friend had told me to wear Nike-branded clothing, but—truth be told—I don't have any. (Maybe that was the first sign I wasn't going to get hired, but I didn't see it.)

Both friends were correct. I saw three guys in suits (walking together), and zero women in suits. All males who weren't in suits were sporting Nike wear, and most of the women were, as well.

I walked from building to building, around the lake, over the bridges, checking out the various employee snack bars, lunchrooms, hair stylists, and little convenience stores—turns out you can drop off your dry cleaning on campus! And why not? There are either 6,000 or 7,000 employees in Beaverton alone, depending on who you ask, and which page of the website you are browsing.

My first intimation that I wasn't going to get hired at Nike happened on that stroll. All the buildings are connected by covered, colonnaded walkways. On nearly every column, and along the sides of many buildings, are a series of bronze busts of famous athletes. Hundreds of busts, maybe a thousand. I walked alone past bronze face after bronze face and . . . I didn't know them. It was a disturbingly dreamlike feeling.

The thing was, in the joy of getting an interview, I had somehow forgotten that I am not interested in sports except kayaking, I have no TV, and I watch no games. In addition to the bronze strangers, I kept passing giant banners with photographs of buff people performing athletic feats. I confess I could not always figure out what the feats were. Something that involved a lot of mud! Something that demanded a swimsuit and a wooden something! I got a little frisson, despite the sunlight, and kept walking.

The lake had a large number of Canada geese paddling in it, and a fraction of the flock was on the brick patio and stairs in front of one building. There was—are you sitting down?—no visible goose poop anywhere. None. It was lovely, and uncanny. The requisite army of goose-poop-removal people was invisible, though I did see a handful of folks mowing and clipping in the distance.

In the interview the next week, I was asked, "What's wrong with Nike, and what would you do to fix it?" I goggled, and said, "I don't know what's wrong with Nike! I don't imagine I'll know until I've worked here a while." This was a poor answer. People who want to work at Nike are expected to be up on Nike. Oops.

After the interview, I was debriefing with a sports-minded buddy, and I mentioned a person I'd met. It turns out she was pretty well-known in the sports world. I had greeted her with, "What did YOU do before you came here?" Oops. I wonder if she's on a column?

But it was a great adventure. I recommend it. I have learned since that there is a book of interview questions hiring managers at Nike use. It tells them what each question is supposed to elicit from candidates. A friend of mine is studying the book this weekend, having been slipped a copy from an insider. I hope he knocks their socks off.

May I Design Your Business Card, Oh, Please?

Title: Software Development Engineer—Parasitic Extraction

Location: Wilsonville, OR

Yeah, My Band Is Called The Business Analysts. I'm on Drums.

Candidate Must Provide Own Microphone haiku:

Job description says

Rock Star! Do we guess they seek

Middle-aged women?

October

Appreciating Mr. 100

The man who turned out to be Mr. 100 in my quest to meet 100 people was an informational interview. (Most are.) I had written him a while back, saying, "I am newly loose on the job market after 30 years in one industry, now trying to meet 100 people in Portland and learn what they do. I got your name from your colleague So-and-So (#78), who said . . ."

He didn't answer. Sometimes I don't ask twice, but I had liked the tone of his website, and the way the organization was portrayed, so I wrote again. He answered, saying he had been swamped, and while he had told several people of my quest and of how So-and-So was #78, he just hadn't had time to write back. So we scheduled a meeting, and yesterday was it.

He asked as soon as I sat down—"What number am I?"

"You are number 100!"

"Okay!" he said, "you're done! You're hired! Go out there and talk to Kay, she'll get you all the paperwork!"

Turned out he was kidding.

He asked what I had learned so far. I said, "Hmmm . . ."

- Portland is a place full of subcultures, and within each subculture, people know each other, but not so much between subcultures.
- There is almost no organization in this town that somebody won't trash. I talk to people, I say I am looking to work for Blah Organization, they say, "Oh, it's SO dysfunctional!" People who don't know me well will nonetheless say things like this.

- So there's not a lot of people being discreet and careful—they're pretty frank and open.
- Actually, one particular nonprofit has been praised by absolutely everyone who mentions it, it is universally mentioned as being well run, so I am trying to get in there and see what they are doing right.

"Which one?" said he. I told him. "Oh, THOSE people? THOSE people are awful! They are just . . . they are like a bunch of piranhas in there!" I stared at him. "Kidding," he said. "I don't know anyone there."

- I love meeting people and learning what they do, and how their organizations work, and what the kinks are. I love listening to people try to explain why they do what they do. I am fascinated by the for-profit/not-for-profit distinction (in reality, and in people's opinions about their sector and the other sector). I am beginning to get a feel for what seems like my next chapter, and what doesn't. I could go on doing this for a long time, if there were some income involved.

We had a great visit; he had lots of good ideas; he loaned me a book and told me to come back again. He was the 100th interview, but the first to loan me a book. Onward!

Milestones, Landmarks, Stats, and Adjustments

Yesterday marked the end of my first 6 months on the job trail.

Yesterday morning, I met Mr. 100, and in the afternoon, I met Ms. 101. They were both great.

In between, I had lunch with Gary, the originator of the concept that if I wanted to change industries, I would need to meet 100 people. I thought it was fitting to meet Gary at the end of 6 months, and at the end of 100 people.

And it was fitting, it was fun, but . . . he had an adjustment for me. Basically, he wanted me to know I was right on track. The goal was 200 people, not 100.

When he had been networking, he had met 200 people. It had taken him a year to find a job. So if I'd met 100 in 6 months, I was halfway there, maybe.

Deeeeeeeeep breath . . . .

Just Wait Patiently. . .

E-mail subject headline from the Portland Business Journal:

"45,000 Executives Are Waiting to Hear From You!"

Go Ahead, Maximize My Day

The job hunt has as many opportunities for self-assessment as some glossy women's magazines: What does the way you wear down a lipstick say about you? Do you keep the little point to the very end? You are meticulous. Do you round down the top? You are practical. Do you flatten the top completely, or chew the edges? You are one odd duck.

So I read the book *Now, Discover Your Strengths*, and took the online self-assessment, and my No. 1 characteristic is I'm a Maximizer. That means (in my case), that when I do something, I don't do it perfectly, but I do it with a whole lot of gusto. I don't do medium. I punch it up.

And my next strongest characteristics are that I'm an Arranger, and an Individualizer. I like to do big projects, with a team, and I like how everybody is different—I like making teams of folks with strong, different talents, and I like getting a lot of mileage out of everybody doing their thing (with gusto). Of course, since my hobby is choreography, we knew all of that already.

On the other hand, a networking friend sent me a link to an article about two types of job seekers: "Maximizers" and "Satisficers."

There was that word again, plus another neologism. In the terminology of this article, Maximizers (in brief) seek the perfect job. They are supremely focused, they know just what they want, they get more interviews, they network harder, they apply more often, and they find jobs that pay more.

Satisficers are less demanding in their job hunt. They have a hard time defining the "perfect" job, and they explore. It takes them longer to find a job. And they find jobs that pay less.

Well.

It seems obvious, at first, that Maximizing pays off.

But here's the deal.

Satisficers are happier with the jobs they find. They report that they enjoy their jobs. The lower pay isn't a primary concern. And they stay longer.

Maximizers, on the other hand, keep job hunting even after they have landed a position. They know they can do better. They report less job satisfaction, and they continue to think about the jobs they interviewed for and didn't get.

In this dichotomy, I'm a definite Satisficer—I have networked with gusto, but it's gusto for meeting people and making connections. In my ultimate job, I could be happy doing a lot of things. When I search, I think: *This job would be good for this reason, and that would be good for another, and they both have their downsides.*

Because I could be happy in a number of roles, I don't really want to narrow my search. I am not aiming for giant bucks, and when I finally find a congenial spot, unless I just make a major miscalculation or things change dramatically, chances are I'll stick around. (I was with my last company 30 years, and with the exception of two short Bad Boss stretches, I loved it.) I'll also do it with gusto. I'll be saying to my new colleagues: *let's improve this here, let's get going, we can do LOTS better, we can be excellent, we can knock their socks off: let's hit it!*

I am in executive networking groups with some pretty high-powered, vocal, job-hunting Maximizers. They preach focus and clarity and narrowing in on some specific industry or organization, some perfect job. They tell me I need an elevator pitch and a one-page leave-behind that lists exactly what I want. They tell me people can't help me if I don't get very, very specific.

I get all defensive and think: Strange, I could swear I'm an executive too, but around these guys, I feel like such a lightweight. Maybe I am just not intense and single-minded enough after all.

So I'm going to satisfice myself around the job-hunt trail, and then when I land something that makes me happy, I'm going to switch into my traditional maximizing mode. This is a gratifying insight. I feel a bit better, understanding it.

Job Posting from careerbuilder.com: Newborn Photographer

Dear Hiring Manager:

As a complete newcomer to photography, I feel my wealth of inexperience makes me well-qualified to contribute to the success of your enterprise. My references (Mom and Dad) can be reached at . . .

November

December
(The Second Year Begins)

Milestone: December 1

- 8 months
- 124 people
- 80 of them people I didn't know 8 months ago
- Many of them very, very helpful, and all of them interesting

Nothing in November

I didn't stop writing entries because I stopped being unemployed. I stopped because this job-hunt advisor told me to stop blogging, that it was keeping me from finding a job. He didn't mean that I was spending too much time on it—he meant that potential employers were ruling me out because I had a blog, and because when they found it, they found me somehow less than desirable.

I protested that it doesn't have my name on it. He maintained that They Could Find It. I thought about challenging him to find it, but then I chickened out.

"They" (the people who could find and disapprove of the blog) are, I guess, the high-powered HR sleuths of giant companies, whose work lives consist of researching candidates and ruling them out. They could also find my Facebook page (which does have my name on it). He had found my Facebook page.

He had found my Facebook page!

He had Googled me, and my Facebook page showed up!

Apparently, he thought that telling me this (more than once) would make me blush. It kind of made me squint, but that was about it. I couldn't figure out what was bothering him.

(I know a lot of HR people, and they all have Facebook pages. I sent out a note to them that night, asking if they look up candidates on Facebook and then reject them. Disturbing note: not one of them answered this question. And they are a pretty chatty bunch. Hmmm.)

Anyway, my advisor advised me to pretty much do everything differently: I should immediately get off Facebook. I should erase the blog. It would take months for my Google hits to clear, but better start now. I should also revise my (beloved) business cards, with a serif font instead of sans serif, and with no graphics and definitely no color, because lots of men are color-blind, and let's face it, men are going to be the hiring decision-makers. I should rewrite my resume. I should really work on my elevator pitch. I should narrow my focus and become CLEARER. People with laser-like focus are the people who get hired first. Laser-like. (He had a penchant for repeating himself.)

The whole encounter left me blue. I took November off. Nobody hired me. I missed my blog.

Milestones and Dreams (No, Real Dreams)

I went to a local pub and joined a Friday-after-Thanksgiving party of former colleagues. I enjoy many of those humans enormously, one-on-one, but the party dynamic was odd: lots of people, lots of noise, lots of shoptalk. Lesson learned—stick to lunches and coffees with one person at a time, or a small, chosen group.

A few days later, I hit the milestone of 1 Year Since I Got Laid Off. (Only 8 months of job hunting, because I gave myself that wonderful 4-month sabbatical and took the Big Drive before I started looking, but still, a year since I worked.)

I dreamt that I walked into a somewhat seedy, florescent-lit classroom, right in the middle of class. There were some charts and graphs we were supposed to understand and discuss. I sat down, realized I was somehow back at work and the old conference room was unrecognizable because it had been enlarged and filled with desks. I could not fathom why I was there, what my role was, but I could tell the charts we were discussing were very poorly printed and hard to see, so I started coloring them in with a tiny stub of a crayon. I turned to a former colleague and said, "I just don't understand why I'm here."

That pretty much summed THAT up.

The following night, I had a rerun of one of my classic anxiety dreams from way back. I was in a play, on stage, with no clue about my role, or anyone else's role, or the plot, or whether it was a comedy or a tragedy. I was trying to respond appropriately to what everybody else said or did, but I really only wanted to get offstage as quickly as possible, and read the script, and figure out what was going on. I actually had a script in my hand, but I couldn't open it up and read it onstage. I just had to get offstage, and I couldn't come up with a reason to exit.

I've had this dream (with many colorful variations, including one where the performance was a sci-fi TV comedy, and I still didn't know my role) at scattered intervals over the years. And though I had a job for 30 of those years running, I still think that THIS time the dream was about job hunting.

This is how interviewing feels: Everybody else on stage has read the script and knows exactly what you should say. They also likely know, already, whether it's a comedy or a tragedy. * You would know what to say if you could just step out of character for a few minutes. But no such luck.

Second Prize Is *Two* Holiday Office Parties!

I did a volunteer stint at a small nonprofit, helping to update some of their literature. It was a pleasure to go in, fire up the computer, and work for a few hours at a stretch, for a few days a week, for several weeks. It was a pleasure to take a lunch break and then go back to my cube. It was a pleasure to get something visible done.

Everybody was very nice, even though I was slightly in the way, as—I gather—volunteers often are. The professor in my nonprofit

---

* FOR INSTANCE, I WAS RECENTLY ONE OF TWO FINALISTS. THE OTHER FINALIST WAS THE WIFE OF A PERSON ON THE HIRING PANEL. I WAS FORTUNATE ENOUGH TO KNOW THIS IMPORTANT FAMILY-RELATIONS TIDBIT, THANKS TO A FRIEND, THOUGH THE HIRING PANEL DIDN'T KNOW THAT I KNEW. I FELT THE INTERVIEW WAS PROBABLY A COMEDY, OR A FARCE, AND THAT I WAS NOT GOING TO GET THE JOB. IT WAS A GREAT INTERVIEW. WE ALL ENJOYED IT A LOT. THEY LIKED ME. THEY SAID IT WAS A HARD CHOICE. AND SHE GOT THE JOB.

management class likes to stress that volunteers are not free. They take time. Somebody has to tell them what to do.

I hadn't been a volunteer before. I hadn't been anything but the boss for many years. It's good to remember what it feels like to be a person without clout or authority. It's good for a recovering boss to remember how it feels to interrupt somebody who really doesn't have time to talk to you, and who doesn't have to pretend it's not an interruption.

The day I finished my stint, the office manager was calling around town, trying to arrange a spot for their holiday party. And as I was leaving, she and the ED invited me to come to the party as well. They said they'd send me an e-mail when they knew the venue. I got a lump in my throat.

Of all the things I imagined I would miss about working, an office party was not on the list. I avoided office parties when I could. So the lump in my throat caught me by surprise. But then, on reflection, not really. What I miss most is being part of a community.

Anatevka

I choreograph high school musicals. I have had the honor to do *Fiddler on the Roof* three times.

Fiddler has this amazing arc, where the first act is nearly all comic, and then the soldiers break up the wedding at the end, and the second act is progressively darker and darker. It's a giant ocean liner of a musical, and somehow the cast has to get the audience to change course, stop laughing, and start feeling their hearts break. Somehow, the kids in the cast need to get the kids in the audience, many of whom aren't used to shows that change in mood, to sober up.

The song where the ocean liner really, finally, has to make the turn is "Anatevka." When we're close to opening night, I give a little talk:

At the beginning, in "Tradition," Tevye talked about Anatevka, where everybody knows who he is and what God expects him to do. It's like being in a play, really, where you know who you are and what the director, and the choreographer, and all of the cast members, expect you to do.

This part of Fiddler *is about how you feel when that ends. It's not about some people in Russia at the turn of the twentieth century who had to move away from their homes. It's about you. You have been in rehearsal for six weeks. You know who you are, and what you are expected to do. You know that the entire show falls apart if one of you misses a rehearsal, or a cue. You know you are important. You know you are valuable, and valued. You know who your friends are, and you see them every day.*

But in SIX DAYS, it will be closing night, and we will NEVER, EVER be together as a group again. Never. Our community will scatter. We will be lonely. We will miss rehearsing, we will not know what to do with ourselves, and homework and laundry will not fill that hole in our hearts. Our community will be DESTROYED, forever.

About this time, the most sleep-deprived girls usually begin to weep. And by opening night, everybody gets pretty misty singing "Anatevka." And the audience comes along.

My former company was sold today. Those friends of mine who hadn't already been laid off will be unemployed in 60 days, or 6 months, some a little later than that. I have been back only twice, to pick up a couple of packages.

Granted, I am grateful not to have worked there this last agonizing year, not to have had to shut it down myself. But there was, until today, a place where a fair number of people I care about congregated. There will no longer be such a place. I will continue to be in touch with the individuals I am fondest of, but the community will no longer exist.

This diaspora happened at the end of college. It happens all the time. I'm a person who puts down deep roots. The breakup of a community makes me grieve.

You're Right. I Can't Complain.

News story on NPR yesterday:

"Conditions have become so bad that X has to share a room with her husband and his first wife, an awkward and embarrassing situation. . . ."

January
(Again)

Required: Minimum 3 Years' Experience Dealing With Dishonest or Corrupt Footwear

Job opening at local sportswear manufacturer:

"Director of Footwear Product Integrity"

Encouragement

I met with a woman today who told me I was three-quarters of the way to my next job. She has coached a lot of job hunters, and was not wearing a headscarf or bangles, and I did not ask her how she had assessed this. I didn't want to burst the bubble. I was simply delighted to hear it.

I then went to my networking group meeting, and told THEM I was three-quarters of the way. I figured they'd appreciate the weird cognitive dissonance, that I am at once delighted and also keenly aware that this is not really data. One of the tech guys said, "Well, yeah, but 95% of the way doesn't get you there." He is, of course, right. Spoilsport.

I then went to a mixer. One of my networking group had said he intended to go to the mixer and speak only to employed people. I laughed at him, said I hoped he could find the two or three employed people who showed up.

Employed people do not attend networking mixers in droves. I'm sure this comes as no surprise to you. And I know why not. It's because mixers are just as awful now as they were in junior high. However desperate and awkward we were then, we are still that desperate and awkward as adults. Only now we need jobs, AND (at the mixers) we can have alcohol, too! So the desperation has a certain fizzy edge to it. I came home hungry and tired, and found myself in a

Scarlett O'Hara mood, shaking my dirty turnip at the indifferent sky, announcing, "As God Is My Witness, If I EVER Get a Job, I Shall Never Attend a Mixer Again."

It felt good. You've gotta have a dream.

Okay. So. Where Were They the Last Time You Saw Them?

Oregon Business headline:

"Portland Metro (Area) Loses 52,000 Jobs Last Year."

Retrospective: Lessons Learned, Part 1

I've been job seeking for as long as it takes to have a baby. Time I produced something! In the absence of other options, I have chosen to produce a list of lessons learned:

Yes, do your homework before meeting people for an informational interview—but beware displaying your knowledge and creeping them out when you do meet. People can be creeped out by an innocent, "Oh, I understand you went to Brandeis!" if you catch them off guard. And then, of course, it's hard to keep the twinkle out of your eye when they say, "I left XYZ Organization to explore other avenues," and you are thinking: Yeah, heard about that.

Conversely, you may think that you are meeting with people you know, or people you don't know, but occasionally you will find that you've met someone who knows you, or knows of you. "I used to work at XYZ, Inc.," you say, and they say, "Yeah, I know Debbie and Terry and Mike and Dan and Kathleen, and I've heard all about you." Creepy, even if your past work life was blameless.

People will generally respond to your e-mails if you got their name from a mutual friend. However, you cannot trust LinkedIn to identify actual friendships. Saying brightly, "I see that you and I are both linked to Joseph!" may bring on a sudden chill, or comments like, "Yeah, Joseph keeps bugging me for a recommendation, and really, he was just average, you know?"

There are a lot of coffee shops in town, sometimes two on the same corner.

When the hiring manager says, "The other finalist is a really good friend of my new boyfriend," it's perfectly acceptable to burst out laughing.

If a job-hunting friend has targeted a company and networked with dozens of people there, it is impolite to refer to him or her as, for instance, a "Yesmail stalker." You want to use the phrase "Yesmail savant."

Some people are extraordinarily generous with their time, their insights, their attention, and their contacts.

Some people give advice with great certainty. That doesn't mean they know you, or know what would work for you.

The Golden Rule can be updated with sobering effect. Rather than "Do unto others as you would have them do unto you," try: "Do unto others as if some day you will need their help finding a job."

Retrospective: Lessons Learned, Part 2

Nobody knows. Nobody knows how to find a job, and if they did, they would tell us, and we would all do whatever it was.

Nobody agrees. There was that guy a few months back who told me to get off Facebook and kill the blog. Last week I spent an hour listening to a guy talk about how crucial it was to be on Facebook, to blog, and to tweet. Furthermore, Guy #2 insisted that we all had to have pictures on our sites, that not having one was equivalent to running around naked. But last month, somebody else said it was crucial NOT to have a picture, that hiring managers HATE pictures and fear that if they admit to having seen ONE, they will be accused of prejudice. Furthermore, the rumor mill says that if you are applying to a government job and you have a picture on anything—LinkedIn, your resume, whatever—they will throw you out of the running immediately just for *having* the picture.

Superstitions abound whenever humans have no control over their destinies. I have sat through a fair number of discussions on whether a handwritten thank-you note is crucial or might be overkill. People seem to think that if they hold their mouths Just Right, if they send Just the Right Thank-You Note, that will do the trick. Me, I just wear my lucky socks. What makes them lucky? Well, nothing, now that you ask.

Fatuous is fatuous. I was at yet another mixer, but better than the last one because all women, so a little friendlier and less full of posturing. One woman asked me how many people I had met on my job hunt. I told her I was at about 150 now. She said, "And have you decided how many you will have to meet before you find a job?" I said, "Two hundred." I didn't mean it. I had not decided anything. I think deciding is idiotic, superstitious, pointless. But I said it, and she said, "Good, because you know, visualization is SO very important." I nodded solemnly. Which leads to the next lesson:

Have an answer. Have an answer ready. Or make one up on the fly. Do not let people catch you without an answer. It might be a stupid answer, but since they probably aren't listening, it doesn't matter much. Just have one. You can say, "I don't know," if you think the other person is actually interested, but otherwise, it's not worth it.

I started thinking about this the other day, and I'm not sure what brought it back into mind. Something. Maybe my weariness with the euphemism "in transition," which always sounds to me like one is perimenopausal. You're UNEMPLOYED. Just spit it out. You're LOOKING FOR A JOB. Sheesh.

Anyway, years ago, I got called for jury duty, and then sent up with a big pool for the voir dire, where they try to screen out anybody who might be biased. There were four questions written on a blackboard: In which part of town do you live? What do you do for a living? Is any member of your family in law enforcement? Have you ever been arrested? One by one, each of us had to answer these questions. It wasn't as if they were a surprise.

The lady next to me, who had seen maybe a dozen people go through the litany already, completely collapsed when she got to "What do you do for a living?" She started off bravely enough, said, "Well, I don't like to think of myself as . . . as unemployed, I like to say (gulp) . . . I mean, I think it's more a case . . . (gulp, sniff) . . . I mean, I really think I'm . . . I'm really more just (sob) . . . between jobs!" Then she put her hands over her eyes and proceeded to weep. The judge dismissed her, and she fled the room.

My thought at the time was, *Wow, you knew that question was coming, and you still couldn't get through it.* I didn't really think she put on the performance just to get out of jury duty.

Hours later, we were dismissed. We filtered downstairs, into the big waiting room where we'd all started our day, and there she was. I was surprised to see her. I thought they'd let her go for the day. And they had, as it turned out, but she had waited. For some reason, she had waited for me. I think I must have made eye contact with her when she had her meltdown.*

She was quite composed. She said, wryly, "I blew it, didn't I?" I said something like, "Well, um, yeah, I think . . . um . . . ," and I raised one eyebrow and shrugged at her, and she laughed, but not like she'd gotten away with anything, just like she saw the humor.

Back in the day, I worked for a company headquartered in Oxford, England. I used to go to Oxford on business from time to time, and I always stayed at a cool hotel within walking distance of the office. What surprised me was that, on my way to and from work, so many people asked me directions. I didn't think I looked British, particularly, or Oxfordian. Then I began to notice that people would actually cross the street, and a busy street at that, to ask me directions. It was weird. There'd be six people walking along my side of the street, and somebody would cross from the other side to ask me—me!—how to get to High Street. But I figured it out. It was eye contact. I was looking at them as I marched along. It was an indication I could be approached. The other people on the street were not making eye contact. I was asking for it.

(True story. One of the people in the Oxford office was a very assertive Austrian woman. She had a cycling mishap on the way to work one day, and ended up in the canal with her bike. The canal was shallow, so she was only wet up to her thighs. She said a number of people walked past her on the path and averted their eyes, so as not to embarrass her by noticing her predicament. She couldn't scale the bank without help, though, and ended up shouting something along the lines of, "Look at me, you jackasses!" This story always cheers me up.)

---

* EYE CONTACT IS A TWO-EDGED SWORD. MAKE EYE CONTACT AT A MIXER, AND GOD ALONE KNOWS WHO WILL GET YOU INTO A CORNER AND START BORING YOU TO DEATH.

Maze or Labyrinth?

The difference between a labyrinth and a maze is that in a maze, you have to make choices about which way to turn. You come to places where the path branches, and if you choose the wrong branch, you will end up, sooner or later, in a dead end.

In a labyrinth, there is one path, which leads to the center, and back out. There are no branches, and no decisions to be made, except perhaps whether to turn around or give up. If you follow the path, one foot in front of the other, eventually you arrive in the center.

There are two local labyrinths in my life, one on the playground of my neighborhood school, and one inlaid in the floor in my church. I walk them when I can. Labyrinth devotees insist there is no wrong way to walk a labyrinth, but I have watched other people do it, and they give off a meditative aura. I am not a meditative type. My mind skitters. But I have noticed that the way the labyrinth is constructed (and you will see this too, if you trace the path), it feels as if you are very close to the center when you first start walking, and very far from the center shortly before you arrive.

I am not at all sure whether the job hunt is a labyrinth or a maze, at heart. I am not sure whether the center is close even when it feels far away, or whether I have gone way down the wrong path and need to backtrack for quite a while. I am not even sure how to backtrack. A view from on high would help, but there's nowhere to get one.

February (Again)

Crazy Jury Duty Lady Lives!

You remember her.

So I have been way down in the dumps lately, as the job-hunt trail lengthens, but I've been doing the get-up, dress-up, show-up drill every day. Today, though, I didn't have to be anywhere till afternoon, and I thought instead of crafting another application or reading websites, I'd give myself a morning off, take a drive, see some countryside, get out of town.

So of course I got nailed for speeding on the outskirts of the little town of Lyle, Washington. I was doing 46. I suspect Lyle's annual budget is augmented by a fair number of people who speed up before they reach the city limits.

I was guilty. I was contrite. I was calm and collected, and then the young, soft cop asked, "Were you out here on business?" and the CJDL suddenly displaced me and in tears I said, "No, rather the opposite of business. I lost my job, and I was feeling sorry for myself, and I . . . just . . . wanted . . . to . . . take (sniff) a . . . DRIIIIIIVE . . . ."

This would have been a brilliant piece of theater if it had been intentional, but it was pure meltdown. He packed me off quickly with just a warning, as one wisely does with the insane.

Coulda been worse. Coulda gotten a ticket, too.

Candidate Must Provide Own Kleenex

My friend Donna just had an interview where the hiring manager asked her if she had ever cried at work. In a fit of integrity, she admitted that yes, though she didn't believe in doing so, she *HAD* cried at work once or twice.

The hiring manager said, "You don't believe in crying at work? People cry here all the time!"

Let it be noted that this wasn't some sort of social service agency where the tenderhearted might be moved to tears at the tragic plight of their clientele. This was a bunch of engineers.

March
(Again)

The Gloomy Science

I just had one of those interviews.

On the one hand, it was enjoyable, because the guy was a CFO, and it made me fondly remember my old CFO, who was just so very practical and data driven. This guy today wanted facts and figures:

- How many people do you know who have gotten jobs?
- What fields are they in?
- How many interviews have you had?
- Why didn't you get hired?
- What are you doing wrong? You should know!
- Is it age discrimination?

By this point, I was saying, "Um, you know, they don't call up and tell you a lot about why they didn't hire you, and they sure don't say, 'We hired somebody fifteen years younger.' And even 'You're overqualified' might be the truth, or it might be something they see as a flattering way of saying no."

"So . . . who knows if it's age discrimination? I mean, when job hunters say they are victims of age discrimination, I always assume the hiring manager was a lot younger than they were. It's a good question, but I don't have much data for you on this."

And the questions were good questions, and the discussion was lively.

On the other hand, it was infuriating. He was a pontificator, full of, "Our economy is doomed; it will never be the same; guys like X and Y (people we both know) will never find decent jobs again," blah, blah, blah.

I said (the first time), "Yeah, you know, I have to not think about that too much because really, I don't need three million jobs, I just need one."

Then he did it AGAIN at the end, after he had already said he would not hire me because I was overqualified. He launched into, "Things will never be the same for middle-aged men who used to make north of six figures. They'll never make what they used to make, and they can't find jobs making less than they used to make, because people don't think they'll stay and won't hire them," and I said (cheerfully), "Are you trying to frighten me? Because really, all you have to do is change the gender, and that's me you're talking about!"

And he STILL would not shut up. He is a Finance person, and he wanted to make this speech about the end of our economy as we know it. (Of course, HE is employed.) So I said (cheerfully), "Oh, you ARE trying to frighten me! Well, it's not going to work! Just so you know! Thanks for your time!"

To his credit, he actually sent an apology just now. For pity's sake! Talk about a tin ear.

Do not tell me I messed up on this one, and my uppity nature lost me the deal. There was no possible deal on this one. He wants a guy. And "We're all going to hell in a handbasket; guys need jobs" is his idea of showing his big heart.

Also, he kept saying "sh*t," as in "I hire guys to put sh*t in boxes."

He wants a guy. I rest my case.

Now I am going to go kick the cat, and then look at other things.

I have no cat, don't worry.

I couldn't work for him anyway. And I'm way overqualified. And this is a family blog, hence the asterisk.

What Makes One Better?

So the Gloomy CFO Who Wants a Guy did send an apology for being "a downer," and I wrote back and said thanks for lunch and the tour and the conversation, and sorry I got a little edgy, but I was just tired from a long job hunt, and his gloom had been too close to home. And he wrote back this morning, said I shouldn't let his opinion have any influence on me.

"Opinions," he wrote eloquently, "are like (and here our family blog shall pause for the sake of any young and/or delicate readers, and use a synonymous phrase) anal orifices. Everybody has one—some bigger, some smaller, some better, some worse."

Renewed by that uplifting thought, it's time to start a new day.

We Have Standards. Don't You Have Standards?

Back in the day, our UK office decided to seek ISO certification* before our US office knew what it was. Suddenly, the UK folks got all doctrinaire about things. And if anything went wrong, they'd call and ask accusing questions. I remember one day asking a formerly friendly colleague what was going on with her attitude. She said, "We have standards. Don't you have standards?"

I thought this was an astonishing display of British condescension. But it turned out to be shorthand. They had to investigate every error very rigorously, in order to prove they could keep their ISO certification. That was what "We have standards" meant.

Well, now I have standards. Nyah, nyah. Only I have the regular kind.

You remember that I chose to use a polite term for Gloomy CFO Guy's simile regarding what opinions are like. The downside of not quoting him verbatim was that he actually misspelled the original word. Really. He put a "w" in it.

Sigh. Verbatim was so tempting. And the high road can be so narrow and rocky.

---

* ISO IS THE ACRONYM USED BY THE INTERNATIONAL ORGANIZATION FOR STANDARDIZATION. IN A DELIGHTFULLY NONSTANDARD WAY, THOUGH, THE ACRONYM ISN'T IN QUITE THE RIGHT ORDER TO MATCH THE NAME, IS IT?

I also wished I had remembered my old boss Doug's wonderful way of responding when things got overly graphic for his taste. Doug would preserve an absolute deadpan, except for pursing his mouth just a tiny bit, and say, "Hmmm. (Pause.) Vivid." And he always made sure to enunciate the v's of "vivid" particularly well.

I did write back to Gloomy CFO Guy. I just sent back that one vivid simile about opinions and wrote, "Hard image to shake."

And of course, I thanked him for his time, and the lunch, once again. I have standards, on the high road.

One of my networking colleagues left his laptop at our last meeting. I'd stayed after to chat with a graduating member, and by the time we spotted his abandoned laptop in the corner, Laptop Guy had gotten way, way down the highway. It was rush hour, so it was going to be a while until Laptop Guy could fight traffic back into town. We called him, asked where he was, and realized it would be a while, so I said I'd either leave it at the front desk or, if they were going to close before Laptop Guy could get back, I'd wait for him. The graduating member went home. I cooled my heels. It was a really nice laptop. I wished I had one as nice.

Eventually, Laptop Guy showed up, thanked me, asked me where I lived. I said I lived over that-a-way. He said he had always thought I lived down near him. (I think the implication was that I might have brought the laptop to a more convenient transfer spot). I said nope, I'm across the river.

He said well, if I lived over there, then why had I met him way the heck south of town that one time when we needed to meet? I said, "Because you asked me to. You live down there. I'm a nice guy."

He said, "You've got to stop that, being a nice guy."

For some reason, this stuck in my craw.

I'd waited for Laptop Guy. I'd met him that other time in an inconvenient coffee shop. And now he was suggesting I was vaguely foolish for doing so. I looked at him and said, "Yeah, it doesn't seem to be paying off so far, does it? But it's going to, I just know it."

Then I went home and muttered, and suddenly decided I was going to ask him for a big favor, the next day. And I did. And he did it. Ha.

Half Full, Half Empty—Who Cares? It's All Fit to Print

My laptop was crashing a lot today, so I got to log in many times. When I bring up my home page, it gives me news from *The New York Times,* so at about 7:00 this morning, the headline was:

No improvement in jobless rate

By mid-day, it was:

Unemployment numbers unchanged in February

And this afternoon, we reached:

Jobless rate holds steady, raising hopes of recovery

Wasn't that fun? It was like one of those sushi places with the conveyor belt, my personal nomination for Best Earthly Example of What Heaven Might Be Like. You sit happily, chatting with your friends and loved ones, while a continually renewed panoply of enticing things parades past you. No struggle. No effort, even. It just gets better and better.

I Guess I Want . . . A Business Problem to Solve

Long ago, I taught in a very isolated school in coastal Washington state. Here's isolated: My commute from the nearest little town to the school itself involved driving 17 miles on a dead-end road that was often one lane wide, because the other lane had fallen into the river. The pavement stopped at the school.

My smartest, cutest, most outgoing, and generally most sparkling senior was Suzette, the eldest of eight children, who lived with her parents and siblings in a barn. They had a cow, which was good, for the sake of the babies. Suzette had big dreams, for a kid from the valley. She wanted to be a hairdresser. She was also thinking of the tiny community college down the coast. One kid from the valley had gone to community college, a while back. She didn't know much about it, but it was intriguing.

I was 22 years old, fresh from student teaching in a downtrodden urban junior high in New Haven. I had one decent lesson plan under my belt, which involved having the kids look at TV advertisements, magazine ads, and billboards, and then analyze the various persuasion techniques employed therein.

Suzette explained that she couldn't do the assignment. There were no billboards on the road down the valley (true); her family subscribed to no magazines; and there was no TV, and—just to be explicit, here—no electricity, in the barn. Electricity could cause a fire.

Then she said, conversationally, since clearly we were discussing entertainment media, "I went to a walk-in movie once."

It took me a second to process this term. She meant a walk-in movie, as opposed to a drive-in movie.

It was clear Suzette thought this was a pretty interesting statement, a lead-in to further discussion. I wasn't sure what my response was supposed to be, so I said, "And? How was that? What did you think?"

She said, "It was creepy. I didn't want to sit in the dark with a bunch of people I don't know."

Suzette spent most evenings in the dark with a bunch of people she did know, so I could see her point. We all get used to what we get used to.

I'm volunteering right now at a local community college with a program called Gateway to College. The program is for kids who have dropped out (or who attend school only very rarely), and who are not likely to graduate from high school. It enrolls them in a special program to help them get their high school degree, and earn community college credits at the same time. It's a great program. The ratio of teachers to students is one to four, the kids are put into small "learning communities," the motto is "no wasted credits," and so forth—it's a whole bunch of good ideas.

My role as a volunteer is to talk to kids at the end of their orientation week, before they commit, and ask a series of questions designed to determine whether they are ready and committed and mature and eager, whether they understand that it's going to be hard work but worth it.

I interviewed a girl recently who reminded me of Suzette, but without the sparkle. She was sixteen, hadn't been to school in ages, had quit in order to help her sister raise a whole bunch of babies. The parents were out of the picture. Until 2 years ago, nobody in the family had ever graduated from high school. It was unheard of. But then her brother did it. And he went through an actual high school graduation ceremony.

Pause.

It was the same pause Suzette gave me, after the walk-in movie statement. I said, "So. How was that? What did you think?"

Well! It was quite something. It was really a bit of a hassle, all the stuff he had to do to get ready for that ceremony. But he did it, and he got to wear the outfit, too: the gown, the mortarboard, or rather—the hat.

Had she been there? Yes! Did anybody else go? Yes, the whole family! They all got there!

She said, "That's what I want. I want to go through graduation." And in particular, she wanted the hat. In fact, her only question for me, at the end of the interview, was whether when she finished the program, there would be a graduation ceremony, with the gown and the hat. I said, "Well, the brochures all have that picture, you know, the kids in the gowns and the hats." She was satisfied.

I don't know if it's a girl thing. I completely understood about wanting the hat. Sometimes you really want the hat. When my kid was little, she wanted the tap shoes. And well before that, when I was about 28, I wanted the car seat. I wanted it so badly, my friend Bonnie let me take her car seat out of her car and drive around with it in my car for an hour. That's what friends are for.

So this girl wanted the hat, and I marked her very high on motivation and told her she was going to make it.

A few posts back, I made fun of the fatuous visualization comment by the lady who thought that if I could visualize getting a job after meeting 200 people, I would get a job after meeting 200 people. But of course, there's a nub of truth in there. I absolutely believe that if this kid can visualize the hat, she's going to get the hat.

Social Networking Wars: Skirmishes to Date

Skirmish 1 was Too Much Advice Guy way back in the fall, who felt that my biz cards were too pretty for any man ever to hire me. "And," he said, "let's face it—most hiring managers are men."

He also said my e-mail address on the cards and resume had too small a period between "gmail" and "(dot) com"—I needed a bigger *period.* He didn't like my font. I needed a font with serifs. Too Much Advice Guy was the one who told me I had to stop blogging because potential employers would find the blog and then not hire me, because of what they saw there. (I assume he meant my uppity attitude, and/or my non-work-related interests. Maybe he thought the blog was too pretty.)

Skirmish 2 was Social Media Guy, who said we absolutely had to blog, or no one would ever hire us. He also said we had to purchase domain names with our names in them, so that when people searched for us on Google, we would be able to direct them from that name search to our LinkedIn profile. So I purchased two domain names. Then I asked him what to do next, so that when people Googled me, it would send them to my LinkedIn profile. He wouldn't tell me the answer, unless we made a deal. Either I paid him, or I let his friend into this executive networking group that I moderate. I got all pleasantly stubborn, told him I'd put his friend on the waiting list.

So I still don't know what to do with the domain names. Somebody in the group today said *SHE* had bought a domain name and just needed to "build it out."

I got all excited, asked her what that entailed anyway. She changed the subject. Now I'm asking her if there's a book I can read. For heaven's sake.*

---

* I HAD ONLY SEVEN VISIBLE FOLLOWERS ON THE BLOG, SO I ALWAYS FIGURED I WAS WRITING FOR THEM. HI, LORI! HI, MARK! BUT AFTER I WROTE THIS POST, MY BUDDY JOE (NOT A VISIBLE FOLLOWER) DROPPED ME AN E-MAIL AND ASKED IF I STILL DIDN'T KNOW HOW TO GET MY DOMAIN NAME TO SEND PEOPLE TO MY LINKEDIN PROFILE. I SAID, "OH, GO AHEAD AND SEE WHAT HAPPENS. GO AHEAD. SEARCH FOR WWW.MYWHOLENAME.COM." I KNEW WHAT WOULD HAPPEN,

Skirmish 3 was a webinar (of course it was a webinar), wherein two Social Media Guys held forth about all the things we had to do or nobody would hire us. They agreed we HAD to blog. Some young-sounding person on the webinar asked what we should blog about, to which the Social Media Guys responded with the usual "blog about what you know; content is king," buzzwords. So the young-sounding person asked if we should blog about job hunting.

NO! NO! Social Media Guys got very emphatic, and they were united in this—Do Not Blog About Job Hunting.

Hey. Tough noogies, Social Media Guys.

This attitude, not the blog, or the size of the period in my e-mail address, or the serif-ness of my font, is probably what's keeping me from finding a job. Can't be helped, though. It's an edgy attitude, but mine own.

Is There Really an "H" in "Wimp" . . . ?

I don't think so.

I get all sorts of e-mails every morning, and it's my own fault, because I signed up for all sorts of job-related stuff—postings, interview advice, online mentoring, seminars, what have you.

Today's mail included an offer to attend a 45-day job-hunting boot camp. The little video of an enthusiastic recent graduate had a crawl across the bottom of the screen, in which the word "itnerview" appeared.

And the ad said the boot camp was "Not for Whimps!"

Not for English majors, either, I guess. Same thing?

Ask me in 45 days if I regret passing this one up. No, don't ask me. Really. Don't.

BECAUSE I HAD PAID $17.95 FOR THIS, AND IT WASN'T PRETTY. HE WOULD GET A PAGE THAT SAID IN GIANT LETTERS:
"NAMECHEAP!
SOMEONE BOUGHT THIS URL, AND IS PROBABLY CONSTRUCTING AN ATTRACTIVE WEBSITE FOR IT RIGHT NOW. PLEASE TRY AGAIN LATER!"
JOE WROTE BACK QUICKLY. "NAMECHEAP. CLASSY." THEN HE HELPED ME FIX IT.

Gifts Along the Unemployment/Job-Hunt Trail

A partial survey:

- 1 bag of apricots, from a lovely man who has an organic-produce warehouse. He said, as we were touring the warehouse, "Do you crave anything?" This sounded both like a complete fairy-tale, dream-come-true question, and simultaneously like a fairy-tale trick question. Didn't Rapunzel get locked up for craving something or other? Anyway, I was brave and said, "Well, yes. Apricots." And he gave me a bag of them to take with me.
- 1 book. When I told another lovely (and very funny) man that I was interested in his field, he handed me a book and said, "Read this, think about if it's you, and come back." What a great way to send someone off.
- 1 invitation to an office Christmas party.
- 1 request to join a nonprofit board.
- 1 chance to run an all-volunteer group.
- 1 very long drive.
- 2 little pots of solid perfume, from a job-seeking friend who landed at a cosmetics company.
- 2 tickets to the ballet (for volunteering).
- 2 tickets to a cool museum (just for showing up to a meeting).
- 2 graduate-level classes with a great professor.
- 2 chances to be in an art show.
- 3 volunteering gigs.
- 4 people I've somehow become ongoing friends with.
- 5 interesting seminars.
- 6 new fantasy careers, more or less.
- 12 new and useful vocabulary words, including the ever-popular "reverse logistics," "individual contributor," "creeper," and "C-level."

- 15 free lunches. (It's a lie. There is such a thing.)
- 30 people I liked so much, I would like to become ongoing friends with them.
- 125 conversations with people I didn't know before I started looking.
- 178 conversations with people who were willing to help me.
- Time. Time off. Bits of free time during the day. Time to sit in coffee shops and look out the window. Time with interesting people who were willing to tell me the interesting things they do. Time to talk to neighbors at the dog park. Time alone. Time to figure out what I wanted to do next.

Headhunt, Part 1: Mr. X and the Mythical Candidate!

I am being headhunted. This is very gratifying.

It's for a job in my old industry. Big job, big staff in several countries, big salary, recruiter is flying into town and interviewing me at the airport next week.

Being wooed, after a long stretch on the job trail, is a grand experience, and I highly recommend it if you have had ego-crushing experiences lately. Mind you, it is unlikely this will provide an end to my job-hunt trail. But it's an excellent diversion.

The recruiter found me in an odd way, by applying to join an executive networking group for which I'm moderator. (What's wrong with just sending a message? Why apply to join a group?)

Fortunately, I wrote back politely (thank you, Mom, for the upbringing), saying, "Sorry, it's a referral-only group, so in order to get in, somebody in the group has to refer you. Do you know anyone in the group already?"

He answered that he didn't want in at all, he was just trying to reach me: He had gotten my name from Mr. X; he was a recruiter; he wanted to send me a job posting; and would I call him, please?

He had gotten my name from Mr. X?

Mr. X gave my name to a recruiter? Really?

There was a time when my beloved old company went through four CEOs in the space of 2 years. It was even more fun than you are imagining it might have been.

Mr. X, who was the second of the four, lasted a few months, then left very abruptly. He called a Senior Staff meeting on a Friday afternoon, swore us to secrecy, and said he would be gone before Monday, because he had been hired by a company (in another industry) that had made him an offer he couldn't refuse.

I remember thinking: *Did he actually just say that?* Why would anybody use a known Mafia-evoking phrase to describe a sudden change in employment?

Well, because. One manager got on the Internet 5 minutes after the meeting ended, and discovered some interesting things. Since the company was publicly traded, he was able to find out what the new employers were going to pay Mr. X, which was a tidy sum. He also discovered why the change was so sudden. There was a small leadership vacuum in the organization, owing to the fact that several of their senior people had just been indicted; it was likely more would be indicted soon.

Oh.

Well.

Sayonara, and . . . best wishes!

I wasn't surprised Mr. X remembered me (we had a few memorable disagreements), but I was surprised he recommended me.

Then I read the job description. What the hiring company wanted the person to *do*, I can do and have done, and I am very good at it. So Mr. X was spot on, and I salute him.

What the hiring company wanted the person to *be*, though, was a possibly mythical beast. Since my old industry is vanishingly small, I must make an analogy.

It was as if they were looking for a professional stamp collector, with a PhD in stamp collecting and a sub-specialty in stamps of 19th century Japan that were cancelled in Hokkaido, plus at least 15 years' experience in a global corporation managing professional stamp collectors who wear only green clothing.

I shall now indulge in blatant stereotyping. Sue me.

In the analogy above, I was trying to find some occupation that might suggest the practitioners were not generally *people*-people. I was trying to find something where, okay, there may be folks like this, but those folks probably don't care to MANAGE other folks. So I wasn't just saying "this is rare," I was saying something like this (who else can I offend today, I wonder): "Looking for a really nit-picky, intellectual, lone-wolf, detail-oriented, introverted, possibly even anti-social type with at least 15 years' experience managing a big team in a global setting."

You see my point.

So I felt a little compassion for the recruiter. I called him up, asked how it was going, and burst into guffaws. I am not sure he saw the humor right away.

Then I said: "Okay. Mr X. was right, and I can do the job, but I don't have the credential, and in my old company, we wore clothing of many colors. I know three people with the credential, and I know one organization in the world where they wear only green clothing. I think you are going to have a rough time filling this exact description, but I may be able to help you a little. Would you like me to pass this posting along to people who might fit, at least in part?"

He said sure, but apply anyway.

So I did both. I had several more phone calls with the recruiter. And I had several jolly conversations with people to whom I sent the posting—it was a good way to reconnect with them. Time passed. Honestly, I pretty much forgot about it.

Candidate Must Not Require Much Salary (and Have Two Friends Who Don't, Either)

Every time this posting pops in my daily alerts, it gets my attention:

"Affluent Operations Manager III"

Headhunt, Part 2: Where Have All the Martians Gone?

One of my best friends is my Continuity in Life (as I am hers). We were in kindergarten together, on the West Coast. We went to summer camp together in junior high. We ended up at college together (on the East Coast). When college ended, we each moved back West, and for a few years there, nobody was making enough money to do any traveling, so we never saw the college buddies. She said to me once, "If it weren't for you, I'd think I had spent the past four years on Mars."

So the headhunting company was looking for an experienced unicorn. Good luck! Time passed; I didn't hear from the recruiter; I pretty much forgot. Then I got a message on my cell phone and an e-mail. The hiring company was interested in me. Would I take an online personality test? (Oh, please.) And then after that, could the recruiter fly out here next week and meet with me, talk about the job?

Sure.

I took the test. He left a message saying he wanted to give me some feedback. I wasn't sure I wanted feedback. The ego-crushing job-hunt thing has made me jumpy. Was he going to tell me my personality was insufficient? Really, *absolutely no need* to bother! Just say they found somebody else, that's enough, honest.

So I called with trepidation, but he's a genuine person, and within minutes I was laughing again. He wanted to tell me that my fit with what they were looking for was "excellent." (Yeah, well, we professional stamp collectors are generally fine folks. All three of us.)

He also wanted to tell me that everywhere he had looked in the industry, he had heard good things about me. Everybody had suggested he contact me, had spoken highly of me. Even people in the hiring company had spoken highly of me, were excited I was in the pool.

I have no idea who these people are.

I don't believe I actually know a single person in the hiring company. Some folks on my staff once met some of them to discuss a joint venture idea that never happened, but I don't think I ever met them. As for those "in the industry" who are not in the hiring company, I suppose they are people I spent 30 years with, on Mars. But I still can't imagine which ones.

Maybe he just talked to Mr. X again, and he's trying to sound like Mr. X is several people. Thing is, I don't want to know who said nice things about me. I want to have a whole bunch of secret admirers. Okay, to be extra-candid, I'd prefer a whole bunch of public, vocal, and local admirers who will hire me in my current hometown, maybe even fight over me just a bit first. But failing that, secret admirers are a good second.

When the recruiter got done buttering me up, I had to ask: "So. How big a pool did you end up with?"

He said he had 10 people, but 5 were not very "mature" in experience. I started to chuckle again. I figure he has 5 people in the industry, plus his next-door neighbor and her 4 home-schooled kids. I swear, there are not 10 people in the country who have much experience in this area.

Before you go getting your hopes up, I just want to say that the job is far, far away, and I don't have any desire to move anywhere. And no, they will not entertain someone based elsewhere. Period. For that matter, I think having managers who are not on-site is awkward, and does not lead to optimal outcomes. But it's nice to be wooed. It really is.

What Part of "I'm Too Superstitious to Talk About It" Didn't You Understand?

When it was my turn in the spotlight at the job-hunt networking group last week, I said, "I'll pass—I've got something in the hopper, but I'm too superstitious to talk about it." I do. I have a new crush, too delicate for public display. And since it was taking a while to go around the circle anyway, nobody argued.

Afterward, when we were straightening up the room, Seth came over and said, "I think this one is going to work out for you."

Seth is very tall. I had a whiteboard marker in my hand, which meant that if I reached up high, I could rap him sharply on the noggin. I did. Twice. Kind of hard.

This is not standard networking group etiquette, and Seth is a big fish in our local networking pond, but when the gods must be appeased, one cannot dally over niceties.

I come from a rich "Do not tempt fate" tradition (and frankly, I suspect Seth does as well). I believe my Grandma Celia would have sanctioned my swift and decisive actions in this emergency, though she generally behaved very properly herself. She would have needed a step stool to accomplish it, but I think she might have whacked him over the head three times, just to be safe. Maybe I should have spit. Too late now.

We Hold These Truths

. . . to be unassailable.

I once had my boss come into my office, burst into tears, and announce that the company wasn't big enough for the both of us. He felt I had outshone him on a project.

I thought he was needlessly distressed and I tried to cheer him—"No, no, you do so many things I never do, everybody values you . . . "

The thing is, though: If your boss says, "This company isn't big enough for the both of us," he's right.

He's right! You will not change his mind, and he is the boss. Put your houseplants in the back seat, and turn in your key card. (I did, but it took me a couple of months. I'm slow.)

Similarly, the immortal phrase "I'm not attracted to you."

I mean, save your breath, right?

And into this august category, let's add "You're overqualified."

There is no convincing counter-argument. All variations on "No, I'm lots less qualified than you think," are a bad idea. All variations on "It doesn't bother me, if it doesn't bother you," fall on deaf ears. And "Just think of me as a bargain" hasn't worked either.

Headhunt, Part 3: What Are We Getting At?

I had a nice two-and-a-half-hour interview with the headhunter when he flew into town earlier this week. I suppose it was all good practice for other interviews I will get (I hope) someday. There were the usual questions: Tell me about some great triumph; Tell me what you liked best; Tell me where you could use some improvement, etc.

What I wasn't expecting was the question, How did you pay for your college education?

We're talking more than 30 years ago, now. He wanted to know: scholarship, loans, or your parents paid? I found this surprising.

Also unexpected: Your maiden name sounds German. Are you German? Well, no, that's an Ellis Island thing. Those folks escaped from the Tsar, during the Jewish pogroms at the turn of the century.

And then there was the perfectly common question: What do you do in your spare time?

"I sing, I dance, I choreograph high school musicals."

The conversation continued, and then:

"What do you do in your spare time?"

The recruiter wasn't a terrific listener—he had already not quite understood a couple of things I'd said. Maybe he was just vamping for time?

Um, besides the singing and choreography, I also take photographs. And I hang out with my husband, and our friends. Sometimes we travel.

That led to more conversation, and then:

"What do you do in your spare time?"

I was beginning to suspect I was flunking this one. Hmmm. The recruiter was from Idaho, and was an outdoorsy type.

I have rafted and kayaked the Salmon and Snake Rivers multiple times! I did 89 miles in a kayak last time, and only tied up to the barge raft when I got really tired and there was a headwind!

He said: "Anything else?"

Of course, being slow, it took me until this morning, three days later, to realize what he was seeking. He was seeking: "I am active in my church."

Here's the funny thing: I actually *AM* active in my church. But I am not used to parlaying that in an interview. And I don't really want to work where I have to parlay that in an interview.

Ostensibly, I'm on the short list and should hear more in a couple of weeks, when the recruiter finishes flying around the country. But my dream is to find work here, where I live already, and where singing, dancing, and kayaking really are enough for most employers.

April
(Again)

Perspective Haiku

Friends and loved ones ill—

Cancer, mental issues, age.

Me? No job. So what?

Myth

On Friday, I had an informational interview at a prestigious local private college. It was a miserable day, with slashing rain and hail, but I left with so much extra time that I was able to stop near the college, have a cup of coffee, and mentally prepare. Then I drove over and discovered, when it was time to buy a parking permit, that my purse was left at the coffee shop.

Oops. Back, grab purse, back to college, park blocks from where the permits are sold, never mind, risk the ticket because being late to an informational is rude, race all the way across campus through the rain and hail to the president's office, dripping and bedraggled but still, miraculously, on time.

And the president is grace personified—finds a spot to hang my dripping coat, seats me in a big brocade chair in front of her fireplace, which is merrily dancing away, offers me tea, and spends an hour helping me imagine how I might serve higher ed. The president and I have two friends in common, which is how I have managed to meet her, but I don't deserve this luxury, this kindness, and all this time. It's lovely. It's the hidden treasure of job hunting—sit in beautiful offices and talk to fascinating people about what they do—and this time there's a fireplace.

When I left, it was 11:30, and I realized if I tried, I could make it to a noon Good Friday service at my church. Why not? I raced back through the rain and hail, all warm on the inside, and drove across town.

Four blocks from the church, I was lined up to make a left in an intersection, and on the sidewalk was a man holding a cardboard sign. He was wet, dirty, and no doubt very cold, and his street-corner misery in the weather was far from my residual fireplace warmth, or even just my dry car. I felt sad, and guilty, and unfairly lucky. And then there was his baffling sign, which read, "MYTH."

I had to think about that. The sign had not always said "MYTH." It had once been bigger. In the rain, the cardboard was disintegrating: The bottom had fallen off, as had the sides. There was part of a letter buried beneath each of his hands. At some point there'd been a word with "MYTH" in the middle of it.

I couldn't think of one.

I made my turn, and got to church. I lacerated myself as a lousy Samaritan, in the bitter certainty that Jesus had been pretty darned explicit about not wanting anyone to drive past a cold, wet, poor man in order to go to church. I realized I'd misread the first letter. The sign had once said: ANYTHING.

Job-Hunt Rules to Live By

Every 45 to 60 days, you should check back in with all the people you have contacted along the job-hunt trail. Personalize your communications, to show that you remember them and something about them. Let them know you are still looking, remind them (briefly) of what you are looking for, and ALWAYS ask them a question, so that you are initiating a two-way dialogue, and they have a reason to respond to you.

Wrong

Dear Fred:

Well, look at that! Another 47 days have gone by, and I'm still looking for an Operations Manager role. Just thought I'd check in with you, and ask: What's the average annual rainfall of the Amazon Basin, anyway?

All the best. . . .

Wrong

Dear Fred:

You and I met in February, in the coffee shop on Belmont. You wore khaki, ordered a tall non-fat latte, and spoke of your fondness for snowboarding and your troubles with your ACL. You like opera and you have little gold flecks in your irises. I wore a very professional-looking jacket in charcoal with a fine pink stripe, and drank orange juice. You said your company would soon be hiring an Operations Manager. So—are you going to do it? And how am I supposed to know? And if you haven't filled the job already, will you contact me? If not, why not? What did I do wrong? What in God's name do you people want?

Sincerely yours. . . .

And Also Wrong

Dear Fred:

You and I met in February, and I was captivated by your statement that the most expensive human enterprise is war, and the second most expensive is opera. It seemed profound, at the time. But I've thought about it since, and it can't be true. What about moon launches? What about the hadron collider? What about the bailout of the banking industry? Or the filming of Lawrence of Arabia, with all those camels and stuff? Opera is the second most expensive by what measure—dollars spent per minute of the final performance? I seriously doubt it. Don't you think you need an Operations Manager to assist you out of your gullible and romantic tendency to accept unbelievable statements like this, and come up with some reasonable way of monitoring things?

Call me. . . . I'm still out here!

Cast Your Bread Haiku

They didn't want me.

Referred a friend, who got it.

Heaven points? No tears.

For Karin

Ain't No Sunshine in the Networking Group When She's Gone haiku:

Comrade lands a job!

Triumph, after twenty months!

Who else gets my jokes?

Today's Brow-Furrowers

Headline in the Portland Business Journal:

"Tillamook Farmers Are Studying Whether Cow Carcasses Can Be Used for Generating Energy"

Go Over It With Me Slowly. . . .

Went to a pretty interesting presentation where the speaker promised to send us some materials afterwards if we would give him our e-mail addresses. Jammed up in the crowd waiting to leave the room when he finished speaking, I noticed the woman next to me wasn't clutching the little "Here's my e-mail" slip. I asked her if she hadn't found it worthwhile.

"No," she said. "We had to give up e-mail."

"You did?"

"Well, it's expensive. We're out of work. We can't afford it. We had to give it up."

"Wow," I said, thinking of the technical issues. "How are you job hunting without e-mail?"

"Oh," she said, "I'm only looking for volunteer work."

Where You Sit Is Where You Stand (and Wag) Haiku

When I'm back to work—

When I get up, shower, leave—

The dog will be sad.

You Should Ask Eric for Some Tips Haiku

Cousin lands a job,

But doesn't tell me himself.

Had to hear from Mom.

Sobering Opportunities From This Morning's E-mail

Mixed Signal Manager

Human Trafficking Intern

Dean of Student Inclusion

. . . must have personal experience with racial, ethnic, gender, sexual identity, and (and?) disability issues.

May
(Again)

Things I Wasn't Grateful for Until Just Now

Heaven knows, we've all got our problems to deal with. Or, as my friend Frances used to say, "Life is maintenance." (I always found this phrase comforting.)

But then, there are problems we don't have, and we don't really stop to appreciate those enough. For instance . . .

This morning, Gmail's little pop-up advertising bar is offering me the services of a bat exterminator in St. Paul.

Headhunt, Part 4:
All's Well That Ends Well

The end (not that the phone has rung yet, but it will) is that I could tell I wasn't really their first choice, nor were they mine, so the whole "Should I move?" thing isn't going to be a problem. I got a great trip, and a bunch of good interview practice, and I heard wonderful music.

Can't do a haiku about this one, or even a rousing gospel number, but a ditty did spring to mind:

Tennessee

Is not to be,

Which is truly fine with me.

Click Here to Stop Liking This Item

I have probably been given this offer by Facebook numerous times, since I am not averse to clicking the Like button (at which "Unlike" appears as an option). But for some reason, tonight it struck me as being one of those things that would be useful in Life. You like something. You like it too much. (I don't know, let's just pick something like, oh, candy.) You want to stop liking it. Click here!

(You would be amused at the amount of time I spent choosing "candy" and the many alternatives I considered and rejected.)

And "like" covers so much ground. The Unlike button could be very useful for eliminating the pointless, lingering crush, for instance. Click here to stop mooning stupidly over this item.

Several job-hunting friends have commented repeatedly on the aptness of the dating/job-hunting analogy. (Yes, they are all female. Interesting.) So the Unlike button could also help turn off the pointless, lingering crush on the job you didn't get, or the company you have networked into, now, umpteen times, and yet they still don't see that they simply have to hire you.

And then, too, couldn't we all occasionally use a Click Here to Stop Resenting This Item button? Click Here to Stop Worrying About This Item. The possibilities unfold. . . .

Click!

How It Happened

I have found Finance recruiters/placement agencies. And I have found a bunch of IT recruiters/placement agencies. But I have not found anyone who specializes in placing Operations people. Or if I have found them, then, faced with the strangeness of my career path, they have pretended not to be Operations placement people when they met me. Hard to say.

But a couple of weeks back, someone told me I should go talk to DH, who had gotten his Operations job through an Operations recruiter, and who therefore must know one Operations recruiter, if not several. So I asked DH, who is the new Executive VP of Operations at a big warehouse south of town, if he'd be willing to meet with me, and he said yes.

I got there an hour early (having written in my calendar when I should leave home, rather than when I should arrive). I hoped to locate DH's admin and find out if I was early or on time, but I couldn't even find the front door, let alone the admin, and so I came in the back of the warehouse, where a nice fellow took me straight to DH. DH was very accommodating about my being there early, told me to sit down, and got out his stack of business cards, so he could point me at Operations recruiters.

Of the four names he gave me, I had already met two, and they hadn't said they placed Ops people, hence my comment above about "pretending." But as he looked, we chatted a bit. DH had spent 27 years with one company. I had spent 30. Each of us had been unable to get anybody in another industry to look at us as managerial (since we didn't know the industry), and had been unable to get a mid-level job because we had the managerial background. We had that in common.

DH had also tried (before my time) to get into the exclusive, referral-only executive networking group that I moderated for 6 months, but he had never come off the (long) waiting list. He was somewhat miffed, since he knew a guy with a nearly identical background to his who had applied after he did, and waltzed straight in.

I had a bad feeling that in DH's eyes I was personifying snobbery, and the worst snobbery at that—the snobbery of one group of unemployed people towards other unemployed people they found insufficiently "executive" or insufficiently "networked." And I *was* personifying all of that, because, to be truthful, that's the reputation of the group in question—they're proud of their executive pasts and their networking prowess. And they've got a waiting list. And not everybody gets in.

So I just said, "Well, here's the thing: It's a good group, and I needed a group, but I can't say they have been spectacularly helpful with leads or connections, to tell you the truth. I think it's mostly me—I am good talking to people one-on-one, but I loathe elevator pitches, and I don't have one that works for everybody, and I don't have a clearly defined path or role I'm looking for. I tend to craft while I'm chatting, based on who I'm talking to. And I can't say why the former moderator let the other guy in and not you, but I'll tell you this: I let some people in because they bugged me, and I didn't let other people in because they bugged me. It was a lot of personal whim."

For some reason, this was the right answer. DH said he wasn't sure he wanted to be in the group anyway, and I said it was a mixed blessing.

Then DH began to talk about how much he loved his new job, and how much he had to do, and he asked me how I had gotten into the building, and I confessed I couldn't find the front door, so I came in through the warehouse. And he said, Yup, he had about a million little projects he couldn't get to, like a sign indicating where the front door was. And then he said he thought he might call up Archie (pseudonym for a guy we both know from networking), and see if Archie could use a part-time, temporary job, doing a few projects for a few months.

Archie is a really nice guy. He's been looking for work for a while. I like him. He deserved the opportunity. Still, I was sitting right there.

I didn't yell, *What am I, chopped liver?* I wrote down the names of the recruiters, and we chatted a bit longer (he'd had an interesting run-in with a customer that morning), and then I said, "Um, what are you going to ask Archie to do?" And he started naming a bunch of small projects, and I looked a little bit abashed, and winced, and just put my hand up in the air like I wanted the teacher to call on me, and he said, "Oh, okay."

So then for a few days we negotiated pay and time (he suggested four days a week, so I can keep hunting—in other words, he's not planning to keep me).

And I did the drug test (lifetime first), and I signed the agreement, and woo hoo! If nothing goes awry, I shall have a short stint (2 or 3 months) of actual paid employment. My resume will not end in 2008. And my obituary will not say, "She never worked again." I am absolutely thrilled at the reprieve, however brief.

But I still felt guilty, having swiped this from Archie, who is a fine fellow. But guess what? Archie got a job last week! A real, full-time, permanent job, at the company he has been courting all along! So everybody is happy!

It is the ritual of the exclusive networking group that when you land, you need to bring refreshments for everybody else, and tell your story. I spent this morning making cookies and will now take them to the meeting. Archie is bringing beverages, because we have the same bon voyage/last day in the group. I shall tell my story, but probably not every single detail. You understand.

Woo Hoo! The Journal of Un(der)employment Studies!

I-Have-Been-Walking-Uphill-for-Over-a-Year-I-Have-an-Unknown-Distance-to-Go-but-at-Least-This-Is-the-First-Bench-Along-the-Trail haiku:

Yippee! I got a

Temporary part-time job.

Starts next week. Thank God.

The Terrible Allure of Patterns

I've been working on graduate courses since September, partly to convince people that I was a learner-bee, and partly because I'm good at school, and by going to school I could get an A, which I sure couldn't get on the job hunt. I'm a person who needs an A every now and then.

Anyway, as a student, I hear from the university a lot—they want to send me health tips and ask me about the cafeteria fare and invite me to various events. I just got invited to the University Diversity Forum. I very much want this wonderful idea to expand. Can't we have a University Diversity Triversity Forum? Can't we? Please?

Irony Counter Runs Riot Once Again

We told our stories (mine abbreviated). We stood up to bid the group farewell (once you have a gig, even a temporary gig, you are no longer in the active group). And one person of the entire group was moved to give me a good-bye hug.

Yes, it was Archie. Bless his heart.

Temp Job Starts Tomorrow—Milestone Time

So what did it take to land the temporary job?

- Participation for 10 months in 1 weekly, 1 monthly, and 2 quarterly networking groups. I also attended about 6 other groups sporadically.

- A 1-day course certifying me as a Supply Chain Analyst. Three quarter-long graduate courses.
- Uncounted applications and cover letters.
- Face-to-face meetings with 207 people, 155 of whom were people I didn't know when I began networking. Most of the meetings were informational interviews.

I met (among others):

- 35 people in Education-related jobs.
- 14 people in Finance.
- 14 in Food.
- 19 in HR, Recruiting, or Consulting.
- 48 in the Not-For-Profit realm.
- 20 in Art or Music.
- 15 in IT.

The temporary job is, I suppose, on the edge of Food. But really, it was just being in the right place at the right time.

Thirty-one of the interviews were not informational, and had to do with trying to land 23 actual jobs. The interview that resulted in the temp job was supposed to be informational, and I broke the ironclad "Never ask for a job at an informational interview" rule. Actually, I broke it a few other times, but not quite so baldly—mostly along the lines of, "So, from what I've said, can you imagine any role for me here?"

I am compelled to concede that the number 207 is extremely close to 200. Gary the former CFO told me it would take 200 meetings to get a job. I don't think he meant a temp job, but still. And you will recall that I responded to the Visualization Lady by saying I was visualizing getting a job when I had met with 200 people. I said it in order to give her an answer, not because I meant it. But there you are.

I suppose now I have to start visualizing what it will take to get a permanent job. I'll get right on that.

Not tonight, though. Tonight I'm just hoping to sleep a bit. I've got my clothes set out, and my lunch supplies in the fridge, and gas in the car. Woo hoo!

Remember the Christmas Party?

Way back last fall, I was volunteering at the sustainability nonprofit, re-doing their little one-page flyer, when they unexpectedly invited me to the Christmas party, and I was overcome with gratitude and a big lump in my throat. An office Christmas party! Me! They were including me!

What made this weird was that I hadn't ever in my working life attended office Christmas parties with real glee, but rather with a sense of duty. But I'd had the option to attend some festive group gathering, and then I'd lost it because I had no work group, and now suddenly this tiny gesture of inclusion bowled me over.

Well, the sentimental nerves are all a-twang this week, after two days on what one of my friends calls my "joblet." I got a login and password. Awwww! I got a key to get into the building if I arrive early. Awwww! I will soon have a nameplate. Awwww! A nameplate! I got an employee handbook. Surely nobody ever gets misty over an employee handbook. Ha. That's what you thought.

I realize the thrill is going to fade. It's like when you come home from a camping trip and think, *Wow, hot running water!* But for now, each little token of employment is a thrill.

I'm Humble!

Many years ago, one niece (now older, wiser, and much more self-aware) thought she wanted to go into politics. She did all sorts of high school student government and Junior States things, and won a prestigious internship in Washington, D.C.—only one boy and one girl from each state was chosen. She was there a week or two, and enjoyed it mightily. When she got back, I asked her about the experience, and she said, "It was great, and it was really good for me, because now I'm humble! I wasn't humble before, but I needed to be, and I am now!"

Maybe you had to be there. There was something about the zest and gusto of her declaration that made me smile hard and bite my tongue.

But it's not as if she is alone. I'm mildly charmed by how often people declare they've become better people for some experience. I don't believe any of us accurately assesses our own goodness, but then again, these folks aren't wrong, either.

So am I a better person for having been unemployed for over a year? I don't think so. I'm very grateful for my little employment respite. I'm sympathetic to the unemployed, and I better understand the emotions that go with an extended job hunt. But I haven't yet gone hungry, or been unable to pay the bills, and I'm still not sure that if my husband lost his job, I would be able to be as supportive of him as he has been of me. He is by nature a worrier, but he has somehow suppressed that all these months, saying over and over, "It's going to take a while. You are doing everything right." I wish I could know that I will be like him, if and when the need arises.

But I wasn't that kindly and unruffled when he was looking for work last time. When I tell him this, he only laughs and says, "That's because I wasn't trying as hard as you have been." He's a good guy. Even humble, sometimes.

(Formerly) Vice President of Operations, West

The oddest thing just happened. I had the cursor over the Title box, meaning, "What will I title my next post," and it auto-filled.

It auto-filled with the phrase "(Formerly) Vice President of Operations, West." Meaning it auto-filled with my old job title and the word "Formerly." OOOeeeeeoooooo. It was eerie.

After much consideration, I get how this happened. Still, it surprised me. And I think we should all consider how to introduce ourselves thus from now on: "Hello, you don't know me, but I'm (formerly) Technical Assistant Level III." "I'm (formerly) Vice President of Drama Club." "I'm (formerly) Clerical Assistant in the Vital Statistics Department of the state of Oregon." I mean, it's true, and it's what job seekers do daily. We could all do it, be sort of collegial and supportive about the whole thing, make it bad manners to say what you are doing now, and some display of subtlety and etiquette to say what you did once.

I actually revised my resume, only 6 days into the temp job. After all, the joy of the temp job is Something on the Resume More Recent

Than 2008, right? So . . . that means I put it on the resume. It was a weird feeling. And then I sent the resume out, because the temp job is a temp job, part-time, so that I can keep hunting for a permanent job. I had a great first 6 days, but my days are numbered.

Days 1 through 5 were full of small and large triumphs, and I learned a whole lot, and didn't step on any toes too hard, as far as I can tell. Day 6 was trickier: got into some interdepartmental communication breakdowns. And I went to a big monthly meeting, and when the boss said he might hire somebody to research a particular problem, I said, trying to be helpful, "Do you want me to do it?" He said no. I felt a little sick to my stomach, suddenly frightened that I'd fail to shine, and not last even 2 months.

I wonder how long it takes to feel safe. Well, for me, for starters, it takes something that is at least billed as . . . what is the right word? It's not "permanent." Nothing is advertised as permanent. I think at the old company the opposite of "temporary" was "regular." I think I'll start to feel safe some time after becoming regular.

Milestones and/or Accomplishments of May

- I have worked 3 weeks.
- I have done my first photo shoot.
- I have fixed a formula that was giving us bad data, made about 10 spreadsheets, and created 2 very attractive graphs, if I do say so myself. I have explained the graphs to 6 people, and they appeared to get the story the graphs were telling. Remains to be seen.
- I have found the bathrooms and the coffee station and the place you can actually get hot water (which is not the coffee station, oddly).
- I have used both "drayage" and "bushing" in a sentence. (And if the sentence was, "I now know what 'drayage' and 'bushing' mean," so what? It's a sentence.)
- I have gone to lunch with a colleague. (I invited her. It was fun.)

- I have received a paycheck. It is my first paycheck since 2008. I didn't even cry. I just said, "Thanks!"
- I have not (yet) spent the paycheck. I haven't even deposited it yet. My husband suggested I xerox it and maybe even frame it. Direct deposit doesn't work till paycheck number two, so this is a REAL paycheck, not a picture of one. I have it in my purse. I stroke it from time to time.
- I have applied to 2 jobs since starting the temp job (resisting the temptation to Take a Complete Break, which is powerful). I have corresponded with my favorite networking group friends, sent job postings to several unemployed buddies, and recruited 1 former colleague for an opening at my new company. I doubt she'll bite, but the thing is, I tried.
- I have gotten a message from the Company-On-Which-I-Have-A-Crush (COWIHAC). They said they don't have any openings yet, but they do have some questions, and they want to keep in touch. Wow! It was unconsummated—I called back; we didn't connect. We shall see what happens, but my gosh, getting a message from somebody! Heady times. I now have a long weekend in which to bask.

And Monday will be a big birthday. The rest of the nation likes to think of it as Memorial Day, and most years it *IS* Memorial Day, but every 5 years or so, it becomes My Birthday Gift of a Day Off for My Compatriots. This year, it's not just my birthday—it's a day off for ME! I haven't had a Day Off in a year and a half! You can't have a Day Off if you aren't working. I think I'll do nothing of note, as a celebration.

Life is good.

June (Again)

Crush Update, Temp Update

The CEO of the Company-On-Which-I-Have-A-Crush met with me Monday and talked about a new business venture they hope to start in July, on which he thinks he could use my help. It's not anything I've done before, but it's very interesting, and I would very much like to be used.

He invited me back in today to meet with one potential partner in that venture, so I am getting all dressed up again, sort of. This is my seventh visit to the COWIHAC, so I've run out of new outfits. However, I did buy brand-new shoes for visit #2, which was the low point in visits so far, and I'm determined to do better than that, so the superstitious behavior of today is: I'm wearing OLD shoes. They're presentable, but they're old. What do you think? Will that do the trick?

At the part-time temp job, I remain delighted to be employed and paid, and to have a place to put my love for fixing processes that aren't working and for getting stuff done. However, yesterday I endured a bracing session of constructive feedback from the boss. I haven't had such a bracing session of constructive feedback in years, since (let's face it) for several decades, I've been the boss. And that's the trouble, here, basically: I'm not the boss, but I keep acting like it.

This being my blog, where I don't have to abase myself unduly, I shall stick to the main point of the constructive feedback (I got to wince at the colorful examples in the privacy of my boss's office, so I really don't need to parade them to you, but you can supply any colorful, wince-worthy examples you like). Let's just say the general thrust was Lighten Up, Slow Down, and Stop Pushing People, Will You?

That's not at all unexpected. I could tell I was pushing people. And I know that in real life, getting people aligned and comfortable and on board is the only long-term road to success. I guess one problem is that I thought this wasn't real life, this was a temporary project management job, and my role and goal were to push people to complete a whole slew of things, within 2 months.

On the first day, I was handed a list of a couple dozen tasks, and next to each task there was a name or two showing who I should work with to accomplish the task. I'd go to the person in question and say, "X is on my list, and I'm supposed to work with you on it," and they'd flinch and say, "It's already on my list! I just haven't gotten to it!" Then I'd laugh and say, "Yeah, but since it's on mine too, I'm supposed to help you. How can I help you?"

Anyway. You see the situation. Not a set-up guaranteed to succeed, but that's how it's been. I thought, I guess this is what it means to be a temporary project manager—it's really a glorified name for Bugging People. Okay, I can bug people with the best of them!

We've gotten a lot done in 5 weeks. But I have been pretty . . . uh . . . pushy.

Anyone who has ever worked with me will be grinning about now, because this behavior is nothing new. I am not deferential, and it wasn't hard for me to push. It's just that bosses get away with pushing, and non-bosses don't. I have never actually developed my No-Authority-Just-Influence-and-Charm skills for getting people to do things. Drat. I should have developed those by now.

Horror Story

NPR has been doing a series on the "jobless recovery," and particularly on people who have been jobless a long time. They interviewed one man last week who was around the 2-year mark. He was—at least in the interview—pretty well put together, matter-of-fact, doing what needed doing, not curled up in the fetal position. He was walking his kid to the bus each morning, and remembering to enjoy that. But at the end of the interview, almost as an aside, he said, "I've lost so many friends, though."

All the little hairs on my neck stood up.

I feel so much sadness for those who have lost more than their jobs. But that's sadness, and this was dry-mouthed terror. He lost FRIENDS. It's my deepest fear. Not my deepest fear about job hunting. My deepest fear, period. You can be afraid of snakes if you want. I won't judge you.

I had to stop and do a quick inventory. Have I lost friends? No. I really haven't. I mentioned the scary NPR story this weekend, when a group of us were together, and I thanked my buddies for sticking with me through all of this. One of them said, well, it *WAS* kind of hard to complain about her work in front of me, this year. And I can see that. But I didn't lose her—she was just self-censoring for the cause. (She may have feared I'd say the dread, "At least you HAVE a job." I might have said it, or exuded it, though I hope not. As my wise friend Dana taught me long ago, misery is relative, and my misery doesn't make your misery go away: My lack of a job doesn't actually make your job any more bearable.)

My buddies and I wanted to know why the guy in the interview lost his friends, but that wasn't in the story. So we speculated about it. Maybe his social life had revolved around the local tavern, or some expensive hobby, and he couldn't afford to go any more. Maybe his friends had all been work friends. Maybe . . . actually, after that we ran out of ideas. I suppose maybe his friends just didn't know what to say.

COWIHAC Comes Through!

Old shoes.

Who knew?

The secret is—wear old shoes.

The Company-On-Which-I-Have-A-Crush came through with a job offer. I am still having trouble believing this is true. But yesterday I heard from the lady who does admin stuff, with questions about my parking-pass needs. And then I heard from the IT guy, with questions about my computer needs. (I said: a keyboard that isn't incredibly loud, please.) And today I heard that I'd passed the background check. I have no background to speak of, but (in jest) the CFO kindly said they'd overlook the moving violation from 1998! Am I lucky, or what?!

I remember that day! I was on my way to the airport! I got in the wrong lane at the traffic circle and pulled a no-no to make the exit to the airport. And then there I was—not only pulled over and in danger of missing my flight, but ALSO getting my first moving violation EVER, spoiling a lifelong clean slate. I was crabby.

I made the flight, I got to the conference, it was late, I was hungry, and I was stomping down the street outside the hotel, trying to find someplace that would feed me, when I ran into a colleague. He asked how I was, and I said, LOUSY, I'm hungry and I got my very first ticket EVER, today.

He beamed, and said, Oh, GOOD!

He was one of those people who has decided he is a Law Unto Himself, and this was just the sort of aggravating thing he WOULD say, so I snapped, Oh, good, WHAT?!

And he said, "It's good you got a ticket. Women who have never gotten a ticket are insufferable."

For some reason, that cheered me up. I have a strong tendency towards insufferable, so it seemed like a tiny bit of insurance. Also, I confess, it seemed like a window into his life. I suspect he had a lot of tickets, what with being a Law Unto Himself. And I suspect his wife and daughters may have had clean slates.

(Let me further digress, here. On 9/11, this colleague was in a plane that was airborne during the attacks, but landed very shortly thereafter at Heathrow. All passengers were told to wait in some secure spot, until they were cleared to leave the airport. My colleague bragged that he had snuck out by going through the baggage claim window as if he were a suitcase in reverse, and then hailing a taxi and getting on with life. A Law Unto Himself. I rest my case.)

Anyway.

Two weeks until I start. Fingers crossed it doesn't unravel or evaporate. The temp job will go another week, and then I'll have a week off. Trying to decide what to do in that week, as a fitting capstone to this journey. I started off the whole unemployment gig, many months ago, with The Big Drive—went to 8 national parks, drove 4,000 miles. But I had time. What to do in 1 week? Mexico? Clean out the closets? (No.) Take a Chinese immersion class? Something. . .

My husband asked if, now that I've landed, I will spend my last un(der)employed weeks filling in the blog with all the job-hunt dirt I didn't want to publish before, this being a small town and all. I was appalled. No, no, no. No dirt. Sorry, but (a) there wasn't much dirt anyway, and (b) if I had dirt, I wouldn't publish it. I feel bad enough for some of the kvetching here already.

Anyway, the good Lord willing and the creek don't rise and the job doesn't evaporate, it's 2 weeks or so, and then the *Journal of Un(der)employment Studies* will need to come to a graceful close—and I hope with all my heart that it can stay closed for a while.

Advice Allergies

One of the networking groups has invited me to present my "lessons learned" from the job hunt, now that I have (knock wood) landed a non-temp job.

I have listened to some of these "lessons learned" presentations, and they are a good opportunity for the presenter. They have that formal, official feel to them, and they mark a rite of passage: A hurdle has been overcome. "I survived!"

I'm not sure they do much for the listeners, except maybe give them the chance to fantasize about what they might say when it's their turn.

It seems to me they are all the same speech. There is a "thank you to those who supported me" section, often with a nod to the divine. I have been sending thank-yous out, and have many more to do. It will take me . . . I can't even guess how long . . . to thank everybody I need to thank.

There's invariably a "hang in there" section to encourage those still seeking work. This usually includes how long the speaker was looking for work, how many times it all looked rosy and then fell apart, and how You Never Know when it will come together. If any drama is to be had, the drama goes in here: I had collected my last unemployment check; I had moved into my parents' basement; I had a bad rash and no health insurance. It's all true, and scary, and sometimes it may make the listeners either feel better or feel less alone.

In between there is the "how I did it" section. This always has a "get up, get dressed, get going" piece, and then a methodology piece (stuff like: "I e-mailed, networked, and sent out applications 6 hours a day Monday through Thursday, and 4 hours every Friday, and didn't eat lunch on Wednesday until I had sent out 3 applications. I exercised for 45 minutes every day. I wrote a follow-up note 57 days after meeting each person, and I included a link to an article I thought they might find useful. I hired a production company for $1,000 to make a video of me explaining why I ought to be their next CEO, and I had a special box made with their logo on it, and I mailed it express mail. . . ." For the record: This is not my methodology; I'm just aping the sorts of things others talked about that made me feel stodgy, poor, and tired.)

I'm chewing on what I should say because honestly, I am not sure what my lessons mean to anyone else. I am not convinced that what I did is a prescription for success, and I am allergic to smugness right now. I don't want to give a methodology that just makes people feel exhausted, or defeated, or unfit. I mean, I'm sociable, didn't know what I wanted to do, and decided my "strategy," such as it was, would be meeting a couple of hundred people. But there are many folks who cringe at the thought. Shall I tell them how to meet a couple of hundred people? Then they can go home and curl up in a ball and weep.

When I think about the Lessons Learned that I've heard, only a few of them really made me feel better, stronger, bolstered up for the journey. One was a woman who said, "You have to protect yourself from negative things, and if that means you stop talking to people who make you anxious, then you just stop talking to them." I'm grateful to her. I felt like she gave me permission to say no, permission not to be nice to everybody at every moment. That was the hard part of job hunting, the imperative to be charming and pleasant. Bleeah. Spare me.

As the recipient of advice, I spent much time in a state of cognitive dissonance. On the one hand, so many people in the job hunt seemed to be so darned Sure of Themselves, and Sure of Their Strategy, and so darned eager to give me advice, even when I hadn't asked for it. Maybe they knew something. Maybe I had to take what they said to heart. And on the other hand, I was acutely aware that those same people were Still Unemployed. So . . . not to be rude, but their advice wasn't exactly working, was it?

Also, often it just didn't sound like me at all. The elevator pitch, for instance. I never got one together that fit all situations. I made it up every time. I hated feeling glib or facile—I'd read up on people before we met, I'd watch their faces and see what they responded to, and craft as I went—which meant I couldn't do an elevator pitch to a group, just to one person at a time. But the guys in the groups would tell me my pitch to the group was no good. Well, so what? You know? The group wasn't going to hire me.

I don't think I can turn in a Lessons Learned speech that says, "If other people's lessons don't seem useful, just ignore them. Smile, nod, love yourself, and do what works for you." But it's sort of what I want to say.

Meeting People Methodology Anyway

I wasn't going to indulge in I'm-such-an-expert How To lessons, but then I met this nice woman yesterday, in town for 1 week, brand-new to job hunting (moved here as her job of 14 years ended), and she was just All Ears. So I thought, *What the heck, maybe this will come in handy for someone.*

Should you decide you don't know what to do next, and you don't know much about the organizations in your locale, and you just don't know enough people who aren't from your last company, and therefore you will go out and meet a whole bunch of people as a part of your job hunt . . . should you decide that's what you want or need to do, here's a little template:

I defined meeting people as talking to them one-on-one for a decent period of time, say 20 minutes to an hour. Most of my meetings were face-to-face, most in coffee shops, but a few in people's offices.

To ask a stranger for a meeting, I didn't call. I am stiff on the phone, and if it were me, I wouldn't really want to receive a phone call in the middle of the day (or night). I'd want an e-mail. So, Golden Rule plus self-serving (always the best justification), I sent e-mails.

Subject line: I got your name from Blank.

(Since I had gotten everybody's name from somebody, this was true. I always got permission from Blank to use his or her name.)

Message:

It varied, but the gist was always something like this:

Hi, my name is X, and I am on a quest to meet people (in town, in education, in the nonprofit world, etc.). I've been working in one company for 30 years, and I just didn't get out much, and I'm trying to educate myself about what other people here do and how they do it. I was talking to Blank today, and she (suggested you would be a good person for me to meet, suggested you know a lot of people in that sector, suggested you could steer me towards worthy and interesting organizations of that sort, said you had decades in that industry before you retired, said your organization was a wonderful place). If you have the time for lunch or coffee one of these days, I would love to meet with you. And if you are just way too busy, I understand.

I think possibly 2 people in the 200-some I wrote to did not answer. Possibly 2. Everybody else either agreed or said, "Sorry, I'm just slammed."

I met with them. I read up on them (if I could) beforehand. I came up with some short version of my story, and told it. I asked them what they did, how it worked, and how it was going these days. Some gurus would tell you that you must ask something incisive and bold, like "What are your biggest business challenges these days?" and then you must use that opportunity to showcase how YOU, yes, YOU could help them solve that challenge. My life-threatening corn allergy meant I couldn't do it—too horribly corny. And besides, if somebody did it to you, wouldn't you just want to smack them? And wouldn't you call up your old friend Blank afterwards and say, "Hey, come on, no more ambushes from desperados, please!" I sure would.

The methodology morphed with each person, and morphed over time. Sometimes their story was so cool, I'd just keep asking questions. Sometimes they wanted to switch it to me, so I'd explain that I had figured out what my oddly disjunct interests were (Food, Education, the Arts, Women's Stuff, Organizational Development, Distribution) and what my turnoffs were (expanded list: Alcohol; Tobacco; Firearms; Porn; Gambling; Spam; Shoes; Cosmetics; incredibly dysfunctional, rigid, or hierarchical organizations; and Books).* Once I'd been around a lot, I'd sometimes whip out my cool

---

* BY AND LARGE, I FOUND THAT I LIKED THE PEOPLE WHO RESPONDED, "WHAT'S WRONG WITH ALCOHOL?" I WAS TICKLED BY

Venn diagram of the organizations in town that interested me, and say: "I've actually been into most of these, but maybe this picture will help you think of one I should look into."

Or—very late in the game—I would whip out my list of the zillions of people I'd met, and say, "Who else should I meet?"

I'd try to notice if they were looking at their watch, and excuse myself promptly. And if they were congenial (most were), somewhere near the end, I'd say either, "Can you think of somebody else I ought to meet?" or, "If you stumble across anything that looks like me, would you let me know?"

If and when I met with the person whose name they had given me, I would drop them a line thanking them for the connection and saying how much I enjoyed meeting them and meeting their friend/former colleague/Pilates buddy/whatever.

That was about it.

Mental Milestone

Subconscious Begins to Believe New Job Is Actually Going to Happen haiku:

Deep in my attic

Is a box labeled, "Desk Toys."

I should dig it out.

God Said Ha!

Temp job ended (right on schedule), at 9:00 in the morning. I had finished everything on the list. I had a lot of stuff to do south of town, on my way home: Get my husband a birthday present, buy a lampshade, get a pair of pants at the only place that carries those particular pants. But I drove around striking out—nothing retail was open until 10:00.

MY FRIEND SUSAN, WHO RESPONDED, "WHAT'S WRONG WITH FIREARMS?" I WILL ALWAYS LIKE MY FRIEND CHARLES, WHO FELT COMPELLED TO DEFEND SPAM. AND I DISLIKED THE GUY WHO SAID, "WHAT'S WRONG WITH PORN?" BUT HE WAS PRETTY ICKY IN OTHER WAYS.

Well, that was okay. I could get a cup of coffee. Or . . . I was near the church where one of the networking groups had met, and I had 20 minutes to kill. I thought maybe I'd go sit in the sanctuary and just be quiet and grateful for a moment, if the place was unlocked. Except I didn't actually know where the sanctuary was—the job-hunting group met in this other room on the courtyard. I assumed I could wander around and figure it out.

So I walked over, and the church wasn't just open, it was hopping. There were four ladies at the front desk, plus an elderly gentleman whose native language wasn't English. And suddenly I was shy. They said, "Yes?" and I said I used to come to a networking group there, but I'd never seen the church, and I wondered if I could see the church. I failed to say, "I would like to sit in the sanctuary alone if that's okay." I mean, for pity's sake—if you can't say that to a bunch of church people, who *CAN* you say it to? But I couldn't bring myself to do it. "See the church" was as close as I could get.

Mistake. The ladies turned to Mr. Non-native Speaker and said, "Would you give her the tour?" and he beamed. This is a big church—congregation of 1,400, three stories, two separate wings. I saw everything. I saw the kitchen, and the dumpsters. I saw the closet where the bells are kept for the bell choir. I saw every single Sunday School classroom. I saw every office, occupied or not, and if an office had two doors, then we went right through it and out the other side. My tour guide did not greet anyone, just told me all about each spot, and I understood much of what he said. But each time somebody looked up in surprise, I said, "Hi, I'm getting the tour," and they seemed to understand.

After a while I got that "God has a sense of humor" feeling, like this tour-in-lieu-of-contemplation was exactly what I deserved for not simply saying what I wanted. And then I realized what the tour felt like: It felt like I was a new employee, getting shown around. And I was a new employee, getting shown around the wrong organization! Ha! Very funny. My 20 minutes flew right by.

Not Quite as Big a Drive

I thought about a bunch of places in the Southwest. I've never seen Bandelier. Then I decided it wanted to be a drive, not a fly-and-drive, so I made reservations at the Oregon Caves Chateau. Only 23 rooms, and I got one. From there, I'll either go down to the redwoods and over to Mt. Lassen, or north all the way up the Oregon coast, depending on the weather. There are cabins and yurts you can rent at some of the state parks. How cool would that be?

July
(Again)

I'm Sorry, I Have to Wash My Hair Tonight

Two Preambles

We once had a salesman who said he was catnip to his customers. He'd return from professional conferences with tales of tipsy lady librarians pounding on his hotel-room door, like something out of a slightly raunchy chick flick. By and large, I knew these women, and I'd think, *Really? Really?* I took the tales with a little salt.

Then I spent a week traveling with him. It was fun. He was a good travel companion, easygoing, tireless, chipper. I'd traveled with salesmen who alternated between being bright and bookish with customers, and brooding darkly in the car between visits. He wasn't like that. We had a good week.

On the way to the airport, we stopped in a Roy Rogers, and I sensed we were about to have a heart-to-heart. He gave me a shrewd look and pronounced his verdict: "I'm just not your type, am I?"

He'd been expecting me to pound on his door, and oddly, it hadn't happened. I grinned at him and said, "Nope. You're just not my type."

Maybe the conference tales were true. It was clear this was a rare experience.

My mom, bless her, told me when I was small that it was okay if not everybody liked me. She said, "You don't like everybody, do you? That's normal. And some people just won't like you. It's normal. They don't have to like you. They just have to work with you." I am supremely grateful to her for this. It seems to me that an awful lot of people, primarily women, want everyone to like them. Give it up. Ain't gonna happen.

And so with jobs. I went into one place where I met with four bigwigs in a row. Every one of them asked me a variation of one question: "What would you do if you were given an assignment, and you thought there was a better way to do it, or thought you should add something to it, or thought it was ill-conceived?" And then they'd each tell me that in their shop, you were not to question your assignments, just do them exactly as told.

It was a strange motif. I started asking: "So, how was the last person you had in this role?" Well, not so great. She had not followed directions precisely. She had questioned instructions. She had done it her way. "And the person before that?" Not so good.

The fourth bigwig minced no words: "If you take this job and you don't like it," said he, "don't come crying to me, because I told you what it was like."

Don't come crying to me.

Noted. Nobody else along the job-hunt trail said, "Don't come crying to me." He gets a unique star!

I needed a job. I suspected they would call me back to meet the CEO. My husband said, "You don't have to take this one." My friend Alan predicted that if I took it, I wouldn't last a week. No, actually, I wouldn't last 2 days.

So when they asked me to meet the CEO, I bravely said no, thanks, it didn't seem like a good fit. And the nice HR lady said, "That's okay. I understand." Think about her life for a minute. How would you like to do HR at Don't Come Crying to Me, Inc.?

So anyway. Work is work. It's not play. You know that. You are going to find work, and it's not going to be 100% fun every minute. But it's okay to say no sometimes, if they're just not your type.

The Wooing of COWIHAC, Part 1

I've reached the point where I'm willing to believe the job is actually going to happen next week. So what the heck, in the spirit of comradeship, I'll tell you how it happened. You know by now that I don't claim special job-hunt superpowers. This is just the tale of how I found this one. If you find it a long and tedious tale (though I'll try to stay on track), you can either just quit reading, or you can think of it as a metaphor. Long and tedious? That's job hunting!

COWIHAC wasn't my first job crush. I had two earlier: one mildly requited that fizzled, and one that was entirely one-sided. And I was applying all over the place, and doing informationals all over the place. And one day, I was at a networking group meeting, giving my tired elevator pitch, and this new guy said, "You should meet my friend, the CEO of COWIHAC. He's got lots of ideas. Tell him Dave says hi."

This is exactly how networking groups are supposed to work: You should meet my friend the CEO.

I went home and looked up COWIHAC, read their website, went on LinkedIn and found people I knew with connections at COWIHAC, contacted them and asked what they knew. It was all good. The Finance types said they were financially sound. Their customers said they were a good company with good products. I did my due dilligence, and it was thumbs up all around.

So I wrote the CEO—"Got your name from Dave. . . ."

Time passed.

Then the CEO wrote back, said he was out of town, but he wanted me to meet two of his VPs, Ms. Marketing and Mr. Ops.

We met; we liked each other. They'd both been with the company for years, and they liked it and liked their boss. This sort of corporate culture makes me swoon. And—astonishingly—there were four openings at the company, three in Ops, and one in Sales.

They felt the three in Ops were too junior for me, but I'd be good in Sales. I disagreed. Ops sounded just fine.

(I was born without the Sales gene. In fact, one time I was on a Sales call with Bob, and when the librarian asked if our system could do Z, Bob and I answered at the same moment.

Bob: "Yes."

Me: "No."

Then we all had a jolly chuckle, while I blushed.

It was a subtle disagreement, really. By "Yes," Bob meant that if the system could not do it, or could not be tweaked to do it, then we'd figure out some manual way to do it, because we very much wanted the business.

By "No," I meant "No."

And as an Ops person who had to come up with a manual way of supporting any strange thing our Sales force promised to customers, I meant, "Oh, *please,* no.")

I didn't want a Sales job. But they thought I'd be dandy, and they said they'd give my name to the CEO when he returned. And I wanted to meet the CEO, so . . . okay, I'd see what happened.

Fozz-Ghee-Ghee

This woman came to talk to one of the networking groups a few months back, ostensibly about communication, but she was really just asking us all the hard interview questions and then exploding our feeble answers. She'd ask, "What do you say when they ask X?" and some poor schnook would venture a response, and she'd snort and say, "I don't believe you." To the rest of us, "Do YOU believe him? Does that sound genuine to YOU?"

I admired her inauthenticity-detection skills, but no way was I going to answer any of her questions. She was fierce. Late in the session, she asked, "What do you say to yourself when you don't get the job?"

Nobody wanted to touch that one. Silence fell. Finally somebody said, "Get back on the horse?" and somebody else said, "I'm one failure closer to success?"

She looked at us, a bunch of unemployed former hotshots now sunk in despair and self-loathing, and she softened. "Look," she said, "other people are going to beat you up—you don't have to beat yourself up. You have to be your own best friend in this process. You didn't get the job? THEIR LOSS. You didn't want to work with those people anyway."

I thought, Oh, I know her best friend! Her best friend was my roommate once. I miss her!

For a while, I took the advice almost literally. Some setback would occur, and I'd think, *What would my best friend say now?*

Since I have a passel of best friends, I could pick and choose. Did I want the best friend who'd say, "We need margaritas!" or the one who would say, "C'est la vie"? Did I want the one who would say, "Awwww, honey, that's rough," or the one who would say, "They're idiots"?

Then I realized I could actually add to the passel, and include an imaginary best friend in the mix. My friend Wendy's baby brother had an imaginary best friend named Fozz-ghee-ghee. (This odd spelling is to help you understand that the G's are hard. Fozz-ghee-ghee's name was never actually spelled, to my knowledge.) My imaginary best friend did not wig out if I wigged out. She did not get worried if I wanted to pull a full Bridget Jones, put on "All By Myself" and crank up the volume for a big, snot-covered weep fest. Fine with her! She wasn't sufficient, of course—I needed real humans to talk to. But she added a lot, and she came in darned handy in a pinch.

The Wooing of COWIHAC, Parts 2 Through 4

Part 2

I got the invite to meet the CEO, and I figured I'd impress him somehow or other, and he'd at least think of me for an Ops job. Or he'd think of something I'd be good at. I bought new shoes.

The meeting was frustrating. The CEO had only a few minutes—something else was on his calendar. And as his friend Dave had foretold, he had a whole bunch of ideas for things he wanted to do. He started listing them, and I was doing my usual slow processing, where I was thinking: *That's interesting, I wonder HOW . . . ,* but I was still wondering *HOW* on idea #2, and he was already on idea #4, and I wasn't sure if any of the ideas related to me, except the Sales job, which I was pretty sure didn't relate to me, though he seemed to think it did, and then he leapt up and said he had to go. I actually said to his vanishing back, "What next?" and he said, "We should talk some more." And then he was gone.

I went home and sulked for 2 days. I called my friends in Sales and asked them if I was a Sales type. They said Marketing maybe. Not sales.

I was entirely out of sorts. I was sure I could contribute. I didn't care if I was overqualified for the Ops job—I'd be terrific at it! I was tired of everybody thinking they knew better than I did.

Then my imaginary best friend observed that if the ball was anywhere, it was in my court. And I thought about all the advice I'd gotten over the months. And I wrote to the VP of Ops.

I said: Hey, we had that great meeting, and then I met the CEO, and it was kind of a dud, and I'm just throwing myself on your mercy now, and asking you two favors. (1) Could you meet me for a cup of coffee, and help me, one Ops person to another, process some of your boss's ideas? I assume Ops people generally start wondering HOW, and I got so lost in the HOW as he was talking that I couldn't keep up. And (2) I want just one chance to persuade you to reconsider the whole "overqualified" thing.

And bless him, he agreed. How nice is that? See, they are good folks.

So we met, and he said he'd told the CEO that we were meeting, and the CEO had said, "Good." And we processed, and I asked for the reconsideration, and he said I could have a panel interview with his team, but if they agreed I wasn't right . . . and I said, "Deal." And he said the CEO was going to be out of town for the next 3 weeks anyway.

Part 3

So I wrote, late that night, to the CEO and cc'd the VP of Ops and said: "While you're out of town, I'm going to take a shot at an Ops job, and if that doesn't work, then when you come back, I'd love to meet with you again. And I know this is really pushy of me, but I want to work there, so I'm just trying to find a way." The CEO wrote back 10 minutes later and said: "Good for you. All I really want are people who give a damn."

More swooning on my part. That was all I really wanted when I was the boss, too.

The next day, I had this revelation. The Ops guy had three openings. Three. I could get at most one of them! I knew some people who would be perfect, from my old company. They were not overqualified. They were ideally qualified. So I wrote to the VP of Ops and said, “I know some really good candidates—may I send them to you?”

And I sent him three people. Because I knew how it was going to turn out. His team was going to agree with him.

Part 4

And that was what happened. They said I was a lovely, smart, personable, experienced type, and I would be good in the company, but not in the roles they had open. And they hired one of my old colleagues.

The Wooing of COWIHAC, Parts 5 and 6

You’re starting to worry now, aren’t you? How many parts are there? Long and tedious. I warned you.

Part 5

So—I didn’t get an Ops job. I didn’t want a Sales job. I had one more chance to meet with the CEO.

I got all sorts of advice, some of it really helpful. I decided to go to that second CEO meeting in a different frame of mind. The CEO was an idea guy. I would arrive with a whole bunch of ideas for things I could do. I forced myself to write it all down in a PowerPoint. I wasn’t going to give the poor man a PowerPoint, but I was forcing myself to be concise and punchy. And I allowed myself to print the PowerPoint and take it with me, in case I went entirely blank.

Great meeting! Fabulous meeting! Terrific exchange of ideas! Meeting of the minds! Laughter! New ideas generated by the sheer fizz! And if anything fitting came up, I’d hear from them!

Part 6

Time passed.

After a while, I decided to drop a note to the VP of Marketing, from that very first meeting. I said: “Hi. I’m still out here. I’ve still got a bad crush on your company. I’m just saying hello, so that if anything happens to come up, I’ll be fresh in your mind.” And she said: “Hi, do you want to come in and talk?” So I went in and talked to her, and she said she'd told the CEO I was coming in, and he had said they they wanted to "keep me engaged."

You know how it all turns out, of course, but I didn't know how it was going to turn out. I was glad they liked me. But I didn't feel like I was really getting any closer to a job. I'd had a crush on them for months.

At the end of the meeting, she told me to keep in touch, and I asked her how often I should drop her a line. Would every 2 weeks be okay? She said sure, she would love to hear from me. And the CEO—should I drop him a line once a month or so? She considered. How about once a quarter?

Once a quarter?! I did not want to be unemployed for several more quarters. You know when they say "that sinking feeling"? I was getting it.

I waited a month before I wrote to her again. Then I said: "Hey, I didn't want you to feel like you were being stalked so I gave you a whole month without hearing from me, but I did want to let you know that I took this temp job, and it has cheered me up no end to be accomplishing stuff and learning stuff, but I'd still rather work with you guys." And she said: "Congratulations, maybe it will become permanent, you never know!" And I said thanks, and sank a little father.

Interlude: You Want Lace With That?

Time for a brief analogy break in our long slog up Mount COWIHAC.

Remember the corrective feedback session I got at the temp job? In addition to the general "back off a bit" theme, there were lots of specifics: You interrupt (I do, it's true); you join conversations without being asked to join (yup, got that from my mom); you invade people's personal space (I do? I don't think I knew that, but it's good to know). It went on like this, alternating home truths, surprising insights, and an occasional mystery remark, where even the boss wasn't sure what it meant. (These were read off to me, not as the boss's own personal observations, but as a long list of comments made about me in a staff meeting I didn't attend. Doesn't that make you writhe?)

Anyway, it was a temp job. I knew I'd been somewhat obnoxious, a lot of the criticism was fair enough, and I was withstanding the ordeal pretty well, until we got to, "You are book smart, but you aren't street smart."

How can I explain my reaction? It was another home truth, so I should have been able to take it like "You interrupt," with a shrug and a sigh, and an admission of guilt. But it is also a "you are" criticism, rather than a "you do" criticism. I can (possibly) change what I do, or try to be more aware of it. But there's not a lot I can do about who I am.

Once, in college, an attractive Irishman who was flirting with my roommate said with scorn (and a killer accent), "American women have no mystery."

Whap! Sound of gauntlet* being thrown down! (Inaudible to YOU, maybe. . . .)

I was determined, on the spot, to become mysterious. Damn it! I would SHOW HIM! Not that he would notice, not that he cared, not that he was flirting with me, but I would SHOW HIM! I would be the most mysterious woman ever!

This plan lasted about a day and a half, before I realized that I have no mystery, I have no desire to have any mystery, and I am not particularly fond of anybody who has mystery. Oh, that's right. Oops. Temporary insanity, sorry.

On the other hand, sometimes people criticize you, or make a tiny little suggestion for improvement, and you have the opposite reaction. You're on a first date, and somebody who looks appealing says, "Have you thought about maybe . . . wearing more leather?"

And you go very still on the outside, because rarely heard parts of your brain are suddenly activated. The place on your cortex designated for impulsive Party Girl thoughts is saying, "More leather? I hadn't

---

* I LOOKED IT UP. IN AMERICAN USAGE, "GAUNTLET" IS NOW THE NORM FOR BOTH THE GLOVE AND THE RAILROAD TRESTLE-ISH THING, AND "GANTLET" IS A VARIANT FOR THE GLOVE. AND "GANTLET" IS ON ITS WAY OUT. BOOK SMART. NOT STREET SMART. DON'T ARGUE WITH ME.

thought of it before, but it's an idea!" And the whole reptilian limbic system is lumbering awake, muttering, "Where are the exits?"

I had all these reactions to "You are book smart, not street smart."

HA! I'll show YOU!

I am street smart! I am DOWN! You ain't seen nothin' yet!

Oh, dear, I must be going now.

I was saved from untold pretzeldom by an old friend who listened to the tale and then said, "Yeah. (Pause.) That 'book smart' thing has been working pretty well for you for a long time now."

It was the scene in the movie where they dump a bucket of water over the person who is raving, and she comes to her senses. Thank you, hon.

A few days later, she said, "Isn't it weird? We are smart, funny, capable, experienced, accomplished adults, and somebody who doesn't know us, and who doesn't really matter to us all that much, can say something that just crushes us?" And I said for me the job hunt wasn't so much about being crushed as it was about being thrown off stride, doubting your own self-assessment, wondering if maybe others saw things in you that you had missed, up till now. I said (back to the theater analogy) it was about not knowing what role you were playing, or were supposed to be playing, or could play. People heard some of what you said, discounted other parts, projected onto you, and gave bizarre advice: Be a nurse! Move to a new city! Why don't you get a PhD? You're a Sales person, you just don't realize it!

Okay, rested up now? Shall we assault the peak?

Woo of Cow Finale

But we HAVE to be getting close to the finale, because I mentioned the temp job to Ms. Marketing! And the temp job didn't last long, now, did it?

A few days later, I got a voice mail from the CEO. He had questions about another company in town that I had mentioned when I was pitching the four ideas. I called; I wrote; we finally made contact in a phone call with a connection so bad he said he'd call me when he got back to town. A weekend went by, and a couple more days, and then he asked if I could come in Monday to talk.

In I went. The receptionist greeted me warmly. She and I were getting to be buds.

The CEO and I did not talk about sales at all, or about any of the four ideas much. We talked about another idea that had floated past in an earlier conversation. He wanted me to come back Thursday and meet a couple of other people. Fine! I'd be there.

So Thursday I met with the CEO and two more people, but after a while, the CEO departed for another meeting, saying he and I would talk details next week, and then the second guy excused himself, and I was there with guy #3, who said the first thing I ought to do on this project was X, and the next thing was Y, and I said: "You know, I haven't actually gotten a job offer."

I was getting sort of worn out. My friend Spencer said I had become a pet, and perhaps soon COWIHAC would adopt me. This was funny, and a little awful. Plus, the temp place had asked me to cover for someone who had left, and he was customer-facing, and I felt I shouldn't be introducing myself to customers if I was leaving, but . . . when would I KNOW*?* So I sent out an SOS to my career lady, Linda, who wisely pointed out that I had pretty much trained everybody at COWIHAC to believe that I would wait forever. And on Friday, I more or less verbatim sent what she told me to send, which was this absolutely charming request for a few "data points" about what was possibly cooking. I sent it to my husband, too, who thought it was the best e-mail ever written. That's because Linda wrote it.

And the CEO said he was planning to offer me a job (aha!) if we could agree on a salary (no sweat), and I went in the next week and we did the world's smallest amount of bargaining, and it was a deal.

Ta da!

See? Piece of cake!

Theme Song Under Credits

Cue the Chiffons! *They're* gonna want me for a backup singer!
www.youtube.com/watch?v=J8LmTaVrPl8

One fine day,

You're gonna want me for your COLLEAGUE!
(Saxophone solo!)

You're gonna want me for your COLLEAGUE!
(Fade out. . . .)

Honor Roll

Liz Adams, Chase Cooper, and Brian Nordwall

Dana Alexander

Meg Amberg

Jane Atkinson

Roberta Avila

Lesley Bain, and Joe, Paul, Ethan, and Allen Iano

Ross Barker

Jason Pearson Bauscher

Kristin Benson

Leslie Bevan

Tom and Stella Bielavitz, and Marisa Schmidt

Rhonda Bishop

Harvey Black

Jill Bleeg

Karl Boekelheide

Keith Bolling

Diane Boly

Tim Bosworth

James Boyle

Barbara Bridge

Rachel Bristol

Lynn Brown

Paul Brown

Holly Brunk

Paul Buchanan

Rita Bueter

Heidi Burgett

Susan Burkett

David Busby

Drew and Lori Callister

Ruth Anne Carlile

Toni Carlo

Linda Carpenter

Christine Carter

Christine Caton

Craig Cedros

Connie Chaplan

Sam Chaplan, and Chuck and Remy Eggers

Matt Chapman

Jill Charvat

Mark Chussil

Mindy Clark

Mike Conley

Dave Cooper

Mary Cramer

Lisa Critchlow

Shirley Cyr

Jana Daugherty

Karen Donovan

Kathleen Doyle

Doug Duchin

Laurel Dukehart

Liz duToit

Dave Dutton

Trink Easterday

Spencer Ehrman

Margaret Eickmann

Liz Erickson

Claire Fay and Kent Robinson

David de Fiebre

Holly Files

Penny Filhouer

Beverly, Lloyd, Lorene, and Chuck Forman, and Shelley Putnam

Holly Forrette

Jan Foster

Damien Francaviglia

Tracy Freeman-Malone

Kyra Freestar

John Frohnmayer

Tom Fuller

Jamie Galbraith

Theresa Garcia and Fred Nilsen

Kathrine Giacchino

Diane Gibson

Lisa Gilmor

Darin Goble

Heather Godsey

Linda Golaszewski

Andrew Gordon

John Haines

Scott Haller

Dan Halloran

Susan Hanson

Amelia Hard

Carol Hausauer

Regina Hauser

Bob Hazen

Jill Hedrick

Jane Hefty

Connie Helleson

Gary Henry

Maripat Hensel

Joe Hertzberg

Ben Hickman

Dan Hill

Bonnie Campbell Hill, and Laura, Bruce, and Steve Hill

Pete Hinck

Josh Hinerfeld

John and Mary Hoagland-Scher, and Irene and Hazel Scher

Terri Hoffman

Amber Holland

Ben, Anna, and Maria Hoisington

Karin Holsinger

Carrie Hoops

Linda Huddle

Brian, Chandler, and Kelly Huotari

Andrew Hutchings

Toni Jaffe

Walter Jaffe and Paul King

Amy Johnson

Kit Johnson

Nina Johnson

Becky Gardner Jones

Liz Joyce

Al Jubitz

David Judson

Nechama Katan

Phil Keisling

Dan Kidd

Jan Kimmel

Kristine Koneck

John Kreidel

Jana LaFrenier

Frances Lau

Rich Lehmann

Mark Long

Melissa Ludeman

Bill Lupfer

Paul Lyons

Shanna Mabry

Doug Martinson

John Mason

Dana Matthews and Doug Hawkins

Anthony Mavricos

Tessa and Nate McClellan

Daniel McClelland

Margaret McGovern

Nanita McIlhattan

Alan, Marne, and Kathryn McIvor

Maggie McNair

Linda Fisk McNeil

Shannon McNerny

Vince Micallef

Seth Miller

Hui Min

Chris Mitchell

Darryl Mollenhauer

Judy Monroe

Regina Moody

Linda Moran

Peggy Morrell

Jim Morris

Dennis Morrow

Stan Muir

Lori Mulcare

Deb Murray

Susan Myers

Julie Nagazina and Richard Einhorn

Laura Nagle

Gary Nees

Sheila Newel

Richard Nixon

Elizabeth Nye

Ryan O'Connor

Scott Olsen

Julie Olson

George Opsahl

Heather Jean Owens

Palio

Dave Patterson

Don Payne

Rick Perry

Candace Petersen

Stacey Philipps

John Pierce

Sandy Pleasants

Jennifer Polver

Quinland Porter

Eric and Toni Price

Mark Price

Vicki Price

Susan Priddy

Brett Pull

David Rabin

Carla Rathbun

Gary Rautenstrauch

Kerry Rea

Jim Rech

Ann Reed

Burke Rice

Brendan and Kent Robinson

Donna Rocco

Mark Ross

Jim Roth

Emily Russell

Bob Schatz

Maryonda and Allen Scher

Holly Schmidt

Bill, Kim, and Susan Schroeder

Rick Schulberg

Natasha Seeley

Bruce Seiler

Debbie Senestraro

Terry Shanley

Greg Shortreed

Mary Sicilia

Michelle Silver

Nick Simas

Joan Smith

Jim Snyder

Kent Snyder

Jeremy Solomon

Gena Spitzer

Gary Squires

Katia and Nathan Steckly

Roxanne Stewart

Stephanie Stoller

Erica Strachan

Katina Strauch

Beth Sullivan

Patricia Summers

Merris Sumrall

Roz Sutherland

Steve Sutton

Cloy Swartzendruber

Julie Talbot

Jonathan Tamez

Janene Thomas and Larry Callister

Tim Thomas

Mike Thornton

Tracy Thornton

Steve and Sally Togasaki

Greg Togni

Tom Tomaszek

Kimi Tomaszek

Carman, Jodi, Kerri, Rylan, and Steve at Traeger

Virginia Tromblee

Mike Urness

Ray Vandiver

Stephanie Vardavas

Gayle Veber

Jerry Vieira

Dale Voeller and Mary Shibley

Janeen Wadsworth

Anne Wagner and Anna Fardell

Idamarie Wagner

Rick Wagner

Ruth Walkowski

Kimberly Wallace

Donann Warren

Liz Wehrli

Jane Weissman

Neville Wellman

Doug Wells

Peter Wendel

Ron Wessner

Ernest White

Barney, Chris, Nancy, Ashley,
and Chelsea at White Bird

Martha Whittaker

Ellen Whitten

Wim Wievel

Amber Wilke

Charles Wohl

Jim Wolfston

David Worsley

Sandy Wright

Bob Yokoyama

Julie Young

Amy Youngflesh

Christine Yun

Allan Bruce Zee

Liz Zenger

Gordon Zander

Debbie Zurow

(Did I forget you? Forgive me.
Thank you to you, too.)

Appendix

Interviews, Interviewers, Why It Didn't Work Out . . .

- Interviews that were related to actual jobs (not purely informational): 33
- Jobs represented by those interviews: 24
- Jobs filled by internal candidates: 2
- Jobs where they said the other finalist had more experience working with volunteers: 1
- Jobs where they said the other finalist was actually the wife of someone on the interviewing panel: 1
- Jobs (different job at the same company where I competed with the wife.!) where they said the other finalist was friends with the hiring manager's new boyfriend: 1
- Jobs where they said I was overqualified: 4
- Jobs where they just said, "We had a lot of good candidates": 3
- Jobs they decided not to fill: 2
- Jobs they might open up sometime later this year, or next year, if they get the money, get the grant, get the business . . . or maybe not: 4
- Jobs I didn't get because on closer inspection, I withdrew: 4
- Jobs I landed: 1 temporary, 1 regular. Woo hoo!

LaVergne, TN USA
14 December 2010

208596LV00003B/12/P